A HISTORY OF TONBRIDGE SCHOOL

CRICKET ON THE MEAD, TONBRIDGE SCHOOL

from an oil painting by C. Tattershall Dodd, sen., 1851

A HISTORY
OF TONBRIDGE SCHOOL

*Nescire autem quid ante quam natus
sis acciderit, id est semper esse puerum*
CICERO, *Orator*, 120

by

D. C. SOMERVELL

FABER AND FABER
24 Russell Square
London

First published in Mcmxlvii
by Faber and Faber Limited
24 Russell Square London W.C.1
Printed in Great Britain by
Latimer Trend & Co Ltd Plymouth

CONTENTS

ILLUSTRATIONS

PREFACE

When my headmaster, Mr. Whitworth, asked me to write this book I applied to the late W. G. Hart, asking him for his assistance on any points of difficulty that I might encounter. Mr. Hart was the most learned of all Old Tonbridgians in the ancient history of the school, as is proved by his editorship of the *Tonbridge School Register*, 1553–1820, and his little volume of essays, *The Old Tonbridge School Lists*. He at once replied that he had in recent years written, for his own amusement, a History of Tonbridge School; that he had given up any idea of publishing it, and that it was entirely at my disposal to use as I pleased: he sent it to me. Such generosity is surely rare and remarkable. It would have been possible to indicate, by inverted commas and footnotes, where I have copied from Mr. Hart's manuscript, and where I have used in my own way material that is common to his book and to Mr. Rivington's *History of Tonbridge School*. But this would be uninteresting and irritating to the reader. Suffice it to say that I accepted Mr. Hart's offer in the spirit in which it was made, and have made full use of his work.

I have already mentioned Septimus Rivington's *History*, first published in 1869, a few years after he had left school, and reissued in a series of enlarged editions, the last being in 1925 just before his death at the age of eighty. To that excellent work I am also greatly indebted, and I should be sorry if any-one supposed that I wished to supersede it. It is a big book, full of detail and of documents, and it seemed that it would be

9

useful to have available a shorter, simpler, and cheaper book for the ordinary reader.

I claim no originality for anything I have written about the history of the school before 1858. In that year the *Tonbridgian* began to be issued. Years ago, over the pseudonym of Metoikos, I published in the *Tonbridgians* of 1922–29 a long series of articles on the 'Back Numbers' of the school magazine from 1858 to 1918. I have now returned to these studies and my narrative from 1858 onwards is very largely based on the ample material which the *Tonbridgian* provides.

A history of a school must necessarily contain estimates of some at least of the men, not all of them headmasters, who have made conspicuous contributions to its welfare. Some of these men, though their active connexion with the school is severed, are still alive, but I felt that this book would be incomplete without some reference to them. Each of them I reckon among my friends and I trust that, if they read this book, they will understand my motives in bringing them into it, and will not take amiss anything I have said about them. They are part of the history of the school and I have written of them, as of historical characters, in the past tense. I have said next to nothing about any present member of the staff.

The headmaster, Mr. Whitworth, has read the book in manuscript, but he read it as a matter of friendly interest and not as a censor. Some one said to me, 'I hear you are writing an official history of the school.' I answered, 'Nothing would induce me to do such a thing.' The book is my own and no one else's. Wherever it offers opinions on what may be regarded as matters of controversy—and it would be indeed a dull history book that ventured no such opinions—no one is implicated except the author.

I. THE FOUNDATION

'And first you are to remember your Founder, Sir Andrew Judde, Knight.

'He was born at Tonbridge, on the estate of his ancestors called Barden, situated by the river-side below Quarry Hill. He was apprenticed in London into the Company of Skinners, and became himself a Skinner and a Merchant of Muscovy. He went with the ships of the Merchants Company, which rounded the North Cape to the coast of Russia. He crossed the country in sledges, a seven days' journey to the River Volga, and so to Astrakan on the Caspian Sea. He also went to the west coast of Africa, to Guinea, at the request of King Edward VI, and brought thence gold dust, to be coined into guineas, and many natural curiosities. In the year 1544 he was Sheriff of London and in the year 1550–1551 he was Lord Mayor, in which office he bore himself with loyalty and valour. On six several occasions he was Master of the Skinners' Company, in the years 1533, 1538, 1542, 1547, 1551 and 1555; in 1554 he was called upon to make a stand for Queen Mary against the rebellion of Sir Thomas Wyatt. He was, moreover, Mayor of the Staple of Calais, and held many public offices of trust under both Edward and Mary, so that he is rightly accounted one of "the worthies of England". He died in 1558, and is buried in the Church of St. Helen's, Bishopsgate, in London, where stands a monument to his memory in marble.

'Five years before he died he founded, not by will but at his own expense during his life-time, besides his alms-houses near

St. Helen's Church, "a stately Free School" at Tonbridge. This he diligently fostered, and framed for it Statutes under which it was governed for 327 years, statutes full of kindly wisdom. Further, he endowed it with certain houses in Gracechurch Street, and with the estate of the Sandhills in the parish of St. Pancras, and afterwards by his will in 1558 with other gifts, whence the School is to this day supported and increased. For all these good deeds, and because this School hath for its Founder so manly and so worthy a gentleman, you shall thank God.'

Every Tonbridgian must recall, however vaguely, the beautiful Bidding Prayer, read annually by the headmaster in the course of the Skinners' Day service in the parish church, which summarizes the main facts of the founder's career. The authorship of the prayer, one of the most distinctive and felicitous compositions of its kind, seems to be now unknown: but it dates from the 'eighties of the nineteenth century.

We must now tell the story of the foundation of the school in rather more detail.

In Sir Andrew Judd's[1] time Tonbridge was a little market town, small even by the standards of those days, with a row of houses nestling under the walls of its Norman castle on the west side of the High Street, and another cluster of houses on the east side with their backs to the churchyard. Besides the castle and the church there was a priory nearly half a mile away to the south of the river. Its ruins were demolished in 1838 to make way for the goods yard of the Southern Railway. Perhaps the town was decaying in Tudor times. It must have owed such prosperity as it ever enjoyed in large part to the activities of the castle and the priory, and the days of both baronial castles and of priories were nearly over. The castle had become forfeit to the Crown and was unoccupied, except perhaps for a royal caretaker, and the shadow of doom was hanging over the priory.

[1] Judd or Judde: both spellings are still in use, for we have Judde House at one end of the town and The Judd School at the other; also Judd St. W.C.1 running across the estate which he purchased for the endowment of the school.

Cardinal Wolsey was seeking means to endow his college at Oxford and in 1524 the Pope granted him a Bull permitting him to destroy a number of the smaller religious houses for this purpose. Among those marked down for suppression was the priory of Tonbridge, and it was dissolved in the following year, eleven years before the general suppression of monasteries by act of parliament. But Wolsey was prepared to give Tonbridge something in exchange for its priory and offered the citizens a grammar school for forty scholars, with endowments enabling the pupils to continue their studies at Oxford. There was at this time, it seems, no provision for education in Tonbridge except such—if any—as the priory had supplied. But Tonbridge had no ambitions. Offered a choice of the school or a restoration of the priory, the citizens opted for the priory and—it was not restored! It was perhaps a memory of this missed opportunity that inspired Sir Andrew Judd to present his native town with what it had refused thirty years before.

Enough, or nearly enough, about the public career of Sir Andrew is recorded in the Bidding Prayer. He was no doubt a more distinguished man than most of the founders of now famous Tudor schools, though not quite as distinguished as his friend and neighbour Sir Thomas Gresham, founder of the Royal Exchange and of Gresham's School, Holt. His home, Barden, is still a familiar item in Tonbridge geography, though the Tudor house has been replaced by one which looks as if it dated from the early nineteenth century. The amenities of the estate have been destroyed by railways which cut through it on both sides of the house.

Sir Andrew evidently figured in that grim scene when the Duke of Northumberland compelled the dying boy King, Edward VI, to leave the crown by will to his cousin Lady Jane Grey, for his signature is among the attesting witnesses of the document. But Tudor-wise, when the plot failed, he found no difficulty in adapting his allegiance and his religion to the requirements of the Catholic Mary, and we find him, two years later, as Lord Deputy and Mayor of the Staple, receiving King

Philip of Spain, Mary's husband, at Calais and presenting him with a purse containing a thousand marks in gold. Hakluyt, the chronicler of Elizabethan voyages, visited Sir Andrew's London house and saw there the elephant's head which he kept as a memorial of his travels—a surprising item perhaps, but Sir Andrew had visited Guinea, and ivory was no doubt among the 'natural curiosities' that he is said to have brought home with him.

In 1553, five years before his death, Sir Andrew applied for and received from the crown a charter for the establishment of a 'free grammar school' at Tonbridge. 'Free grammar school' (libera schola grammaticalis) is the description always used in charters of this period granted to founders of schools, but its meaning has long been a matter of controversy. The popular view is that 'free' implies an absence of school fees, and on this basis is erected the theory, dear to persons of advanced opinions, that the so-called public schools were intended by their founders to play the part now played by state elementary schools and that they have been diverted from this wholesome intention by the machinations of the wicked rich. Evidence in refutation of this view, so far as Tonbridge is concerned, will appear in due course. More probably 'free' implies the status of the school in relation to external authorities and means that its governors, as established by the charter, were to be independent of all jurisdiction save that of the crown.[1] The charter ordains that the governors of the school after the death of its founder were to be the ancient City Company of the Skinners, of which Sir Andrew himself was a distinguished member. In entrusting the government of his school to a City Company Sir Andrew was following the example set by Dean Colet fifty years before for his school of St. Paul's. There are many other cases, and in some of them the school still bears the name of the company, for example Merchant Taylors' School.

---

[1] In what I have written on this controversial subject I follow the guidance of Mr. Hart, dissenting from the view upheld in Rivington's *History*. I make no claim to an opinion of my own but imagine that Mr. Hart, as a lawyer and antiquarian, is the better authority.

Having secured his charter Sir Andrew set about providing for the endowment of the school. He bought for this purpose five houses in Gracechurch Street in the City and thirty acres of pasture-land, called the Sandhills, in the then rural parish of St. Pancras. It is the urban development in modern times of these thirty acres that has provided the school with its magnificent endowment, from which every member of the school, quite apart from scholarships open to competition, now profits to the extent of about fifty pounds per annum. In other words, he receives for about £150 an education which costs about £200 a year.[1]

As soon as, or perhaps before, these financial arrangements were completed Sir Andrew had appointed the first headmaster, the Rev. John Proctor, and began the building of the school. The site of the old school building was within the grounds the school still occupies, along the High Street between the headmaster's house and the building which, once the school chapel, now houses the library. It was an oblong structure in Tudor style, built of the local ragstone and about 160 feet in length, with the usher's house at the northern end, and a bell turret in the middle of the roof. Though it was, most regrettably, demolished in 1863 and replaced by the Ruskinian Gothic building behind it, it is familiar to us all in many agreeable steel engravings. There may indeed be still living a few very aged inhabitants who can remember it 'in the flesh'. For the rest the only stone that survives is the foundation stone, now placed over the headmaster's porch and reproduced on the cover of the *Tonbridgian*. It bears the ill-spelt inscription—

'This shole made bi Sir Andro Jwde Knight and gevin to the Compane of Skiñers ano 1553.'

The charter empowered Sir Andrew to make 'fit and wholesome statutes and ordinances in writing concerning and touching the order government and direction of the master and under master and scholars of the school'. These are the statutes 'full of kindly wisdom' to which reference is made in the Bidding Prayer, though the author of that Prayer was mistaken in think-

---

[1] These figures are appropriate to the years before 1939.

ing that they governed the school for 327 years, i.e. until the new scheme of 1880. They had in fact been superseded by an earlier new scheme of 1825.

The statutes require that the master of the school shall be 'holle of bodie, well reported, Maister of Art in degree (yf it may be) . . . and by examinacion founde meete bothe for his lernynge and dexterities in teachinge as also for his honest conversacion[1] and for right understandyng of Godes trewe relygion nowe sett forthe by publicke authoritie whereunto he shall styrr and move his scollers'. The true religion at the date when Sir Andrew penned his statutes was the Catholic faith as re-established by Queen Mary. But Sir Andrew had been a Protestant once and he would doubtless have approved of his school following the lead of 'public authority' after the accession of Elizabeth. At least he did not, like another pious founder in Mary's reign, ordain that his 'scollers' should say daily masses in perpetuity for the repose of his soul. This they —I refer to the Reptonians—have for nearly four hundred years shamefully neglected to do, their nearest approach to it being the singing of a school song in which they invoke their founder with the words

'Jolly Sir John, you are dead and gone.'

The statutes then provide salaries for the master and undermaster, five pounds quarterly for the one and forty shillings for the other. These seem to have been about fair market rates, identical with those ordained at Harrow, superior to Rugby where the headmaster got only £12 a year, but inferior to Westminster where the headmaster got £39 6s. 8d. But Westminster, a royal foundation, was and long continued to be a school of much higher status than these provincial grammar schools.

There follows an interesting provision[2] 'I desiring the benefit of the inhabitants of the said town of Tonbridge in

---

[1] 'Honest conversacion' means good moral character. Compare the phrase in one of St. Paul's epistles A.V. 'our conversation is in heaven', altered in R.V. to 'our citizenship is in heaven'.

[2] I have modernized the spelling in this and later quotations.

boarding of scholars and otherwise do will that the master of the said grammar school shall not take to board diet or lodge in his house or rooms or otherwise above the number of twelve scholars and the usher not to take above the number of eight scholars.' This seems to indicate that the Founder anticipated and intended that the majority of the boys would be boarders, for the building which he erected appears adapted to accommodate only fifty or sixty boys, which, so far as evidence goes, was a number very seldom exceeded by the school in the sixteenth, seventeenth or eighteenth centuries. Now if the master and usher were to have twenty boarders between them and the people of the town were to have the benefit of boarding a similar number, that would only leave room for about ten day boys. Indeed, so far as it is possible to judge, forty boarders and ten day boys represents about the relative numbers of the two constituents of the school during the first 270 years of existence.

The next important clause ordains that before a boy could be admitted to the school he must be able 'to write competently and to read perfectly both English and Latin'. This together with the clause already quoted about boarders is plain evidence that Sir Andrew did *not* intend to found an elementary school for the benefit of the humble cottagers of Tonbridge town. He founded what we should call a secondary school for the benefit of his own class, the local gentry of West Kent and East Sussex. The benefit he intended to confer on the townsfolk was less cultural than financial, namely, the profits of boarding some of his young gentlemen. Elsewhere in the statutes he exhorts the master to be careful in his choice of households for the boarding out of scholars, and not to entrust them to hosts who were given to 'gaming' or 'lewdly occupied'.

Next we learn how the work of the school is to be conducted. The day was to begin with prayers at 7 a.m., and teaching was to be continuous till 11 a.m. when there was a two hours' interval. Work was resumed at 1 p.m. and continued until 5 or 6 p.m. A 'remedy' (i.e. holiday, *remedium laboris*) was to be given not more than once a fortnight.

Finally the founder gives directions for the ordering of an institution which, with minor alterations, has been maintained ever since, namely, the annual Visitation of the Governors on Skinners' Day.

'Considering that virtue and knowledge by praise and reward is in all estates maintained and increased and specially in youth I will that every year once, to wit the first or second day after May day, there be kept in this school disputations upon questions provided by the master from one o'clock in the afternoon till evensong time, at which disputations I will that the master desire the vicar of the town, with one or two other of knowledge or more dwelling nigh, to be present in the school if it please them to hear the same.

'The disputation ended, to determine which three of the whole number have done best by the judgment of the master and the learned hearers, and I will that the first allowed have a pen of silver whole gilt of the price of 2s. 6d., the second a pen of silver parcel gilt of the value of 2s., the third a pen of silver of twenty pence for their rewards.

'And then I will that the whole company go in order decently by two and two into the parish church, the three victors to come last next to the master and usher, each of them having a garland upon their heads provided for the purpose, and in the church then and there to kneel or stand in some convenient place to be appointed by the discretion of the wardens (of the Skinners' Company, or the churchwardens of the parish?) and master of the school. And to say or sing some convenient psalm or hymn with a collect for the preservation of the queen's majesty. And to have some honourable remembrance of their founder to be appointed and devised by the master.'

Sir Andrew does not actually ordain that the Master and Wardens of the Skinners' Company should attend these ceremonies. Perhaps he did not feel disposed to issue instructions to such exalted persons in such a matter. None the less their attendance has been from the first the outstanding feature of the occasion. As for the inevitable changes wrought by time, the date has been changed from the beginning of May to the end of the summer term; the disputation of a single afternoon has given place to the sterner stuff of a ten days' written examination under Higher Certificate rules: the vicar's share in the proceedings has been diminished to the saying of grace before the dinner annually given by the governors to the visiting examiners and the staff at the Rose and Crown; the service in the parish church precedes the awarding of the pens; the school no longer proceeds to the church in a decent crocodile, and no one is embellished or embarrassed with a garland.

Sir Andrew Judd died on 4th September 1558, having made his will on 2nd September. It is notoriously difficult to make a watertight will, and the fact that in his case the will-making so shortly preceded death suggests haste. Anyhow the will was in certain technical points inconsistent with the legal arrangements the testator had already made for the endowment of his school. These discrepancies provided material for a lawsuit in 1819, more than two and a half centuries later, as will appear in due course.

Meanwhile, and on quite other grounds, the Skinners' Company had to fight for the retention of the school's endowment against a certain Andrew Fisher, son of Henry Fisher, who had been Sir Andrew Judd's servant and co-trustee for the school during his lifetime. Andrew Fisher never had any friends in Tonbridge and he now has none elsewhere, so we will not hesitate to declare that he was forger, a liar, and a thorough rogue—but a most pertinacious one. He kept the Skinners fighting him for the best part of fifty years. They called in the assistance of the Archbishop of Canterbury and the High Court of Parliament and when at last they emerged victorious they had spent the enormous sum (in Elizabethan currency) of £4,000 in the defence of what Sir Andrew Judd had entrusted to their care. By far the greater part, if not the whole, of this sum must have come not from the Judd endowment but from the property of the Company.

Two more paragraphs of the Bidding Prayer recall certain other foundational business with which this chapter may be concluded.

'And secondly you are to remember the grandson of your Founder, the son of his daughter Alice, Sir Thomas Smythe, a great benefactor to the school and to the poor of Tonbridge. He was born about 1558, and dwelt near Southborough. He was for fifteen years Governor of the East India Company and took part in establishing the colony of Virginia. He founded four exhibitions from this school to the universities of Oxford and Cambridge. He died in 1625 and was buried at Sutton-at-Hone in Kent.

'Furthermore you are to remember Henry Fisher, the faithful servant of Sir Andrew Judde, who founded a scholarship at Brasenose College, Oxford; Sir Thomas White, founder of St. John's College, Oxford, who "propter eximium amorem in Andream Judde" gave to Tonbridge school a fellowship, now a close scholarship, at his college; also Robert Holmdon, the founder of the Leathersellers exhibitions, Thomas Lampard, Lady Mary Boswell, Mr. Worrall, Mr. Strong, all of them benefactors of this school.'

Sir Thomas Smythe, Sir Thomas White and Henry Fisher explain themselves. Their benefactions are named and we still enjoy them. But what of these other mysterious persons? Will it be accounted an act of impiety to look their gift horses in the mouth? At any rate let us venture to do so.

Robert Holmdon left by will in 1619 certain property to the Leathersellers' Company upon condition that they paid four pounds yearly to a scholar of Sevenoaks School and, in default of one from that place, to a scholar of Tonbridge school. So far as we know our friends and neighbours at Sevenoaks have never, in modern times, failed to intercept this benefaction.

Thomas Lampard, yeoman of Tonbridge, bequeathed an exhibition of four marks (£2 13s. 4d.) to be awarded by the headmaster to the *poorest* scholar in Tonbridge Grammar School. But, though we have still many poor scholars, the emoluments have long ago disappeared.

Lady Mary Boswell died in 1692 leaving property to furnish two exhibitions tenable at Jesus College, Cambridge. These were, like Holmdon's exhibition, to go to Sevenoaks schoolboys, and, failing Sevenoaks to Tonbridge. It is doubtful if Tonbridge ever enjoyed this benefaction, and in 1877 it was conferred on Sevenoaks outright by the Charity Commissioners.

Mr. Worrall left two small exhibitions tenable by members of Tonbridge School at St. John's College, Cambridge. They ceased to exist after the Universities Commission of 1856, being merged in the general scholarship funds of that college.

Mr. Strong in 1713 left a sum of money 'for the apprenticing to some marine business of a scholar educated at the great School of Tonbridge'. One would think there could be no doubt that 'the great School of Tonbridge' was Sir Andrew Judd's foundation, but the Charity Commissioners decided otherwise and since 1886 the funds have been devoted to two scholarships for boys from, alternately, the Tonbridge National School and St. Charles the Martyr's School, Tunbridge Wells.

These facts are taken from Mr. Rivington's *History*. It will be observed that some of these benefactions have ceased to exist and others, so far as Tonbridge School is concerned, perhaps never existed. But the names of these benefactors are enshrined for ever in the Homeric catalogue of our Bidding Prayer, and who would wish them away? In recent years two further names have been added to the prayer, those of Edward Goggs and George Floyd, assistant masters of comparatively recent date, who founded by bequest prizes for history and English subjects.

II. THE FIRST TWO HUNDRED AND TWENTY YEARS (1553-1772)

In this chapter we shall cover more than half the life of the school from its foundation to the present day, but though the period is a long one it will not detain us long. Tonbridge Grammar School, like so many other schools which rose to national status and renamed themselves public schools after the coming of the railways and the vast increase of wealth and population in Victorian times, was but a small and perhaps insignificant institution in the sixteenth, seventeenth and eighteenth centuries. It may have done its job passably well but it was, in schoolboy jargon, 'nothing to write home about'. At any rate, not much was written that has survived, and much of what has survived is routine matters, recorded in old account books and minute books at Skinners' Hall, diligently combed out and published in Septimus Rivington's standard work on Tonbridge School, but not to be rewritten here except where some real human interest seems involved.

National histories have taken the reigns of kings as a chronological framework, and school histories make similar use of the reigns of headmasters. Many of the earlier ones are mere names, with little or no personality now discoverable. But here at any rate is a list of them, twenty-four completed reigns in all, which gives an average of sixteen years for each reign.

Rev. John Proctor, M.A.	1553-8
Rev. John Lever, M.A.	1559-74
Rev. John Stockwood, M.A.	1574-87
Rev. William Hatch, M.A.	1587-1615

Rev. Michael Jenkins, M.A.	1615-24
Rev. Joel Callis, M.A.	1624-37
Rev. William St. John Newman, M.A.	1637-40
Rev. Thomas Horne, D.D.	1640-9
Rev. Nicholas Grey, D.D.	1649-60
Rev. John Goad, B.D.	1660-2
Rev. Christopher Wase, B.D.	1662-8
Rev. Thomas Roots, M.A.	1668-1714
Rev. Richard Spencer, M.A.	1714-43
Rev. James Cawthorn, M.A.	1743-61
Rev. Johnson Towers, M.A.	1761-72
Rev. Vicesimus Knox, B.C.L.	1772-8
Rev. Vicesimus Knox, D.D.	1779-1812
Rev. Thomas Knox, D.D.	1812-43
Rev. James Ind Welldon, D.C.L.	1843-75
Rev. Theophilus Barton Rowe, M.A.	1876-90
Rev. Joseph Wood, D.D.	1890-98
Rev. Charles Coverdale Tancock, D.D.	1899-1906
Charles Lowry, M.A.	1907-22
Harold Newnham Penrose Sloman, M.A.	1922-39
Eric Edward Allen Whitworth, M.A.	1939-

In this chapter we will cover the period from Proctor to Towers inclusive.

Proctor, the first headmaster (1553-8), was no doubt selected for the post by the Founder himself, and his reign coincides with the remaining years of Sir Andrew's life. Both died in the autumn of 1558. Proctor was a Roman Catholic and wrote a history of Wyatt's rebellion, that futile demonstration of certain gentlemen, mainly Kentish, against Queen Mary's proposal to marry Philip of Spain. He also wrote two volumes of theological controversies, directed not so much against contemporary Protestants as against heresies of the early Church: from which we may conclude that our first headmaster was a studious and learned man. He was also a Fellow of All Souls College, Oxford, and Sir Andrew himself was a great-nephew of Archbishop Chichele the founder of that college, and nominated the Warden of All Souls in his will as

23

'Advisor' of the Governors. His advice has seldom if ever been sought, but our connexion with this eminent and unique institution (the only college in any British university which does not allow itself to be pestered by undergraduates) still persists in the fact that the annual examiner in classics for the award of the Judde exhibitions is usually a Fellow of All Souls. Presumably All Souls has the first refusal of the office.

Of Lever, Proctor's successor (1558-74) we know nothing directly except an entry in the Skinners' accounts—'the chargis of bringin down the Schole Master, Mr. Leyvar, to Tunbridge with horse meate'. This last was not stuff for feeding the boys but a special allowance to each headmaster on appointment to cover the cost of removal. Indirectly, we gather that the school prospered, for Holinshed's *Chronicle*,[1] published in 1577, after recording Sir Andrew Judd's foundation of the school, says that therein he 'brought up and nourished in learning grete store of youth as well bred in Kent as brought up in other counties adjoining'.

Stockwood held office for thirteen years (1574-87). In his twelfth year he had been appointed vicar of Tonbridge, and the Governors thereupon 'warned him to resign', either because they did not think that two such offices should be combined or because they had found him an unsatisfactory headmaster and took this occasion to get rid of him—a little of both perhaps. Stockwood was a prolific and miscellaneous author, some of his works being translations from the Latin of foreign divines. Among them are *A Short and Learned Treatise on the Plague*, *A Short Catechism for Households*, and *A Bartholomew Fairing for Parents* 'to bestow upon their sons and daughters, and for one friend to give to another, shewing that children are not to marry without the consent of their parents', etc. Stockwood also wrote some grammar books for school use which enjoyed a remarkably long life, one of them being reissued in the eighteenth century. He seems to have been a kindly and humorous person, and one of his grammar books

---

[1] Holinshed's *Chronicle* was the principal source used by Shakespeare for his English historical plays.

contains a dedication to the 'Young Punies and Petitis of the Grammar School' whose fate it will be to study in his book.

We have no registers showing the age of admission to the school in those days, but it may be presumed that, though some may have remained at school till they reached the modern school-leaving age, nearly all will have come to school much younger than the present age of 'common entrance exam'. In spite of the high standards demanded by Sir Andrew in his statutes we may suspect that the sons of socially suitable parents were admitted at a very tender age and with a very slender equipment of learning. There were no preparatory schools in those days, and the boys would come straight from the domestic tutor, if not from the nursery.

On Stockwood's retirement we hear for the first time of competition for the post of headmaster, and of the Skinners' methods of selection. They appointed for the purpose a committee of six of their own number with power to co-opt such 'learned' advisers as they might require. One of the advisers called in to assist the Governors on this occasion was probably the headmaster of Westminster. Hatch was an Old Tonbridgian (the first O.T. to appear before us in these pages) and is said to have been the best 'ebrician' (Hebraist?) among the candidates, and he reigned from 1587 to 1615—or, if you like to be kept in touch with larger events, from just before the Spanish Armada till just before the outbreak of the Thirty Years War. In 1594 the Governors made to Hatch a grant of ten pounds 'in hope of his longer continuance'. Doubtless he was offered preferment elsewhere, and this was a means of inducing him to remain. He remained, or 'continued' another twenty-one years, but they have no recorded history.

During the next headmastership, that of the Rev. Michael Jenkins (1615-24) the school was enriched by the endowment provided by Sir Thomas Smythe, Governor of the East India Company and grandson of the Founder. He raised by 50 per cent the salaries of the headmaster and usher, for prices were steadily rising and the value of money falling at that time, as the early Stuart kings found to their cost. He also founded six exhibitions of ten pounds per annum for seven years to enable Tonbridgians to proceed to a university with a view to taking Holy orders. In awarding the exhibitions the Governors were to take account of the scholarship of the candidates, the poverty of their parents and the length of time the boys had been in the school. A record of the candidates for the first election in 1621 has been preserved, and runs as follows:

'Six boys stood in competition for Smythe exhibitions.

'(i) Thomas Smith, 4 years at the school whose parents are of small abilitie (i.e. wealth).

'(ii) John Dixon, whose friends are of great abilitie and hath continued scholar 1½ year.

'(iii) John Large 1¾ year, a minister's son.

'(iv) Richard Bell 2¼ year.

'(v) John Bullocke 5 year.

'(vi) Geo. Children 5 year, a very poor woman's son.'

The exhibition was awarded to Smith, as he surpassed Children in scholarship. The surnames Large and Children are decidedly uncommon, so it is perhaps worthy of note that both have appeared again in the school list in quite recent years. The Children family was conspicuous in the history of the town through many generations, and the member of that family who was in the school shortly before the Second Great War was almost certainly of the same stock as the 'very poor woman' of 1621.

Sir Thomas, like his grandfather Sir Andrew, made his benefaction in his lifetime. He attended Skinners' Day with the Governors in 1620, when the Rev. Thomas Gataker preached a sermon full of complimentary references which was reprinted with the title *David's Instructer*. There is a copy of this rare and interesting little book in the school library.

His successor, John Callis, was headmaster from 1624 to 1637. All we know of his reign is that there must have been some rebuilding and re-adornment at the headmaster's house. The sundial on the outer wall and the overmantel in the dining-room both bear dates that fall within Callis's reign.

William Newman was only with us three years (1637-40),

being promoted to the vicarage of Coldred and Sheperdswell. Why the Governors voted him the large sum of fifty pounds on his retirement is unknown.

The headmastership of Thomas Horne (1640-9) coincided with the conflict between Charles I and the Long Parliament. There was actually a little battle in Tonbridge, a troop of royalists being driven through the town from north to south by the parliament's men, but as it took place in the summer holidays the boys cannot have seen it. However they were nearer to seeing fighting in 1643 than they were to be again till 1940. Horne was a parliament man and in 1649 a curious exchange took place. Dr. Horne was promoted from Tonbridge to the headmastership of Eton, and Dr. Grey, expelled from the headmastership of Eton for his royalist views was afforded consolation in the comparative obscurity of Tonbridge (1649-60). At the Restoration Grey returned to Eton, not as headmaster but as a Fellow of the College. The two men are buried at Eton side by side.

To Dr. Grey's headmastership belongs the first extant list of the boys in the school. There were fifty-three boys, and at least two of them came of good county families and had distinguished careers ahead of them.

Mr. Goad was headmaster for two years only (1660-2), when he passed on to become headmaster of Merchant Taylors'. The most curious fact about him is that he was, when headmaster of Tonbridge, already a secret Roman Catholic, like his sovereign Charles II. He had been received into the Roman Church in 1660, a fact which was afterwards discovered and led to his expulsion from Merchant Taylors'. However, we are told that he was 'an exceedingly loving and tender man'. He was also, more surprisingly, a meteorologist or expert on the weather. On this branch of science he drew up reports for his fellow-Catholic, King James II, and presented them monthly at the palace. How very curious this is! Did he forecast a whole month's weather, and if so how did he do it?[1]

---

[1] One who claims to know tells me that seventeenth-century meteorologists did not foretell future weather but merely recorded it when it arrived—an easier task.

The next headmaster, Christopher Wase (1662-8) was a friend of the diarist, John Evelyn, who visited the school on Skinners' Day 1665 and records the fact in his Diary. A school list extant for that year shows a large number of county family names, the most notable O.T. of those days being Charles Mordaunt, afterwards Earl of Peterborough, the brilliant soldier and notorious eccentric who captured Barcelona in the war of the Spanish Succession. Wase left Tonbridge to enter the political world as an Under-Secretary of Arlington, one of the members of the 'cabal' ministry.

Ten years after leaving Tonbridge Wase published a book entitled *Considerations concerning Free Schools as Settled in England.* In order to secure first-hand information for this work Wase addressed what would now be called a questionnaire to the headmasters of a very large number of grammar schools. His questionnaire was accompanied by a circular letter from the Vice-Chancellor of Oxford University calling attention to the importance of the inquiry Mr. Wase was undertaking. Large numbers of headmasters replied, and their manuscript reports, bound up in four volumes, are to be found to-day in the library of Corpus Christi College, Oxford. They constitute a unique authority on the state of English education in the reign of Charles II.

During Wase's headmastership there occurred, in 1666, the Great Fire of London, and the minute-books of the Skinners' Company record the following resolution: 'Whereas the houses bequeathed by Sir Andrew Judde for the support of the Free Grammar School of Tonbridge are all burnt down and cannot for some time to come produce any rent, it is hereby resolved that the Skinners' Company shall for the present hold no feasts or entertainments, and shall devote the sum thereby saved to the support of the School.' Whenever we feel disposed to criticize our Governors—and the present writer must admit that he has occasionally heard them criticized—we should recall this noble resolution, and it will doubtless mollify our asperity.

Twice in the course of eight years the Governors had appointed a headmaster who found Tonbridge too small a sphere for his activities and went elsewhere. Perhaps they were determined to avoid making this mistake again when they appointed, as successor to Wase, his usher, Thomas Roots. Anyhow so little fitted was Tommy Roots—surely he must have been called Tommy Roots?—for further promotion that he remained headmaster for forty-six years (1668-1714). The school declined both in quantity and quality. The number of boys fell to fourteen, and year after year the examiners for the Smythe exhibition reported 'there are no scholars fit for the university'. The Governors intimated their wish that the headmaster should resign, but he declined to do so. Under the statutes they were entitled to dismiss him if he became 'a common gamester or haunter of taverns' or 'otherwise an infamy to the school and an evil example to the young', but perhaps his failings were sins of omission only. Anyhow, the Governors did not press the point. It seems likely that Tommy Roots was the worst of our headmasters, and it was in a very low estate that the school entered the eighteenth century. But he probably holds one record; as scholar, usher and headmaster he was within the school for fifty-eight years.

Richard Spencer (1714-43) brought new life to the school and numbers quickly rose to seventy, remaining thereabouts for the next twenty years, and quality at least equalled quantity. Mr. Hart's researches have discovered that at least eight of his old boys either inherited or achieved baronetcies. 'There's glory for you!' as Humpty Dumpty would say. But he seems to have stayed too long, and when he left the numbers had fallen to twenty-six. A pleasing fact about this headmaster is that he gave to one of his sons, born during his headmastership, the Christian name of Skinner. Let us hope that the Governors showed their appreciation in a practical manner.

James Cawthorn (1743-61) was a Yorkshireman and left the reputation of a severe disciplinarian, so severe that his ghost remorsefully haunted the school house dormitories for more than a hundred years afterwards. Elderly O.T.'s alive to-day can remember the tradition. The version I have been told is that Cawthorn locked a boy up in an attic as a punishment and then forgot all about him. After an unspecified interval of time he recollected the unfortunate youth while out riding, started to gallop home, fell and broke his leg. The boy was subsequently found in the attic starved to death. The only element of truth in the story is that Cawthorn did in fact die as the result of a fall from his horse.

During his reign the headmaster's dining-room, officially still called 'the Skinners' Library', was built to house what was then the school library. Some of the more valuable and interesting books of this collection are now in glass cases in the present school library. The rest still repose upon and cumber the shelves of the headmaster's dining-room.

Cawthorn was a poet in the established style of his generation, the rhyming couplets of Alexander Pope, and he composed versified orations to be recited by the pen-winners on Skinners' Days. The subjects of these compositions do not strike us as appropriate to the occasion: 'Lady Jane Grey to Lord Guildford Dudley: an Epistle in the manner of Ovid'; 'Anne Boleyn to Henry VIII: an Epistle in the Manner of Ovid'; 'Life unhappy because we use it improperly, a Moral Essay'; and least appropriate of all, 'The Temple of Hymen'. A quotation from the first of these effusions gives a fair idea of the style.

> *From these dark cells in sable pomp array'd*
> *Where night's black horrors breathe a deeper shade*
> *Where ev'ry hour some awful vision brings*
> *Of pale assassins and the shrouds of kings,*
> *What comforts can a wretched wife afford*
> *The last sad moments of her dying lord?*
> *With what fond tear, what love-impression'd sigh*
> *Soothe the dear mourner ere he reach the sky?*
> *Ye powers of song that ev'ry chord inspire*
> *When Rome's soft Ovid weeps along his lyre;*
> *Ye angel sounds that Troy's great Hector mourn*
> *When his lost consort bleeds upon his urn;*

Teach me, ye warblers! teach the strain of woe
Like you to kindle and like you to flow.

After Cawthorn's death a collection of his poems was published by subscription, most of the subscribers being his own Tonbridge pupils. The volume is in the school library, and can occupy an idle hour very pleasantly.

Three O.T.'s of Cawthorn's day are worth mentioning. George Austen, Smythe exhibitioner and afterwards usher or second master, survives only as the father of the most perfect of English novelists. But Jane was not born until after her father had left Tonbridge for a country living in Hampshire.

William Woodfall, who recited 'The temple of Hymen' in 1760, was one of the pioneers in the illegal practice of reporting parliamentary debates. He was known at school as 'Memory Woodfall'. Mr. Cawthorn set him one evening a book of Homer to learn by heart. The next morning Woodfall repeated it word for word, and the headmaster 'was so affected that he burst into tears'—though whether he added 'it hurts me more than it hurts you' is not recorded.[1] Less than ten years after he left school Woodfall was parliamentary reporter for the opposition newspaper which published the letters of *Junius*. His practice was to secure, by arriving long before the time, a good seat in the House of Commons and then, with no more food than a hard-boiled egg secreted about his person, he used to sit for eight or a dozen hours, storing the debates in his memory, for no note-taking was allowed. No other journalist equalled Woodfall in the fullness and accuracy of his reports composed under these harassing conditions. A few years later the efforts of John Wilkes secured the right of journalists to report the debates of the House of Commons and Woodfall's peculiar gifts were no longer required.

Another distinguished O.T. of this period was Lord Whitworth, British ambassador in Paris during the brief period of the treaty of Amiens. When Napoleon wanted to break the

---

[1] If Woodfall was allowed to choose his book of Homer, he would choose the shortest, about 300 lines. If Cawthorn chose it, it might be anything up to 900.

treaty he publicly insulted Whitworth, which would surely be
an honour for any Tonbridgian. In fact Whitworth was treated
by Napoleon very much as Sir Neville Henderson was treated
by Ribbentrop in similar circumstance 136 years later.

An incident of this time is worth recording, not for any light
it throws on Tonbridge school, but as an illustration of the
ways of the world in the reign of George II. It was 1759,
Pitt's famous year of victories—Quebec, Minden, Quiberon
Bay and the rest; and in the course of these triumphs King
George II conferred a baronetcy on Sampson Gideon, a Tonbridge boy of fifteen who had reached the fourth form. Why
was this?—because Sampson Gideon the elder, father of the
above, had made himself very useful in financial matters to
Pitt's business manager, the Duke of Newcastle. Sampson
Gideon the elder was a Jew, but Sampson Gideon the younger
was a little Christian, as how should he be otherwise with all
the advantages of a Tonbridge education? So S.G. the younger
received the baronetcy that S.G. the elder had earned. The
letter of S.G. the elder to S.G. the younger has been preserved
and should be reproduced here as a model for the guidance of
parents placed in similar circumstances.

Dear Sampson,

The King has been pleased to order his letters patent
to promote you to the dignity of a baronet; it is the lowest
hereditary honour but the first step. I have hopes that by your
own merit you will go higher; I shall otherwise wish his
majesty had not been so generous.

I have always recommended to you the practice and title of
an honest man; that only will render you honourable with the
wise and good, reconcile your conduct to yourself and be
acceptable to God. You are allowed to charge your coat with
the arms of Ulster which are in a field argent a hand gules; let
them be a constant warning before your eyes that if ever you
sign a bond, paper or instrument, derogating from truth, your
duty to the king, or destruction to your estate, that very moment
you commit a crime as much to be detested as a hand of blood.

Behave, my dear boy, as you have hitherto done towards your master, schoolfellows and everybody. Remember the old proverb, 'When pride cometh then cometh shame, but with the lowly is wisdom'. Johnson in his farce points to the vice strongly—'Pride is an adder's egg laid in the breast of every man but hatched by none but fools'.

Mama, Lord and Lady Gage and sister join in joy and love to you.

Your affectionate father,
SAMPSON GIDEON.

Show this with our compliments to Mr. Cawthorne, then keep it clean till you come home.

S.G. the elder evidently thought well of this composition and hoped that both Mr. Cawthorn and posterity would agree with him.

The next headmaster, Johnson Towers (1761-72), is the last whose reign falls within the period covered by this chapter. Cawthorn had brought the numbers up to sixty again, and there they remained for some years but fell to forty before death terminated Mr. Towers' headmastership.

During these years a dispute arose as to the extent of the area within which the inhabitants might claim free education for their sons, apart from entrance fees and extras, if they passed the statutory entrance examination already mentioned. The Governors referred the matter to certain eminent lawyers, among them the greatest legal writer of the age, Sir William Blackstone, and received the opinion that privilege extended to all inhabitants of the parish of Tonbridge. This was a wider area than the ordinary person might suppose, for the ancient 'civil' parish of Tonbridge included most of the surrounding villages and also Tunbridge Wells, a place which simply did not exist at all in Sir Andrew Judd's day but was by 1760 already a larger place than Tonbridge. This question of the geographical area of Sir Andrew Judd's benefaction came up again later on as we shall see.

We possess a letter from Johnson Towers to the bishop of

Rochester, which throws an interesting light on the kind and quality of the school at this time. The bishop had evidently written inquiring about Tonbridge school on behalf of some parents who thought of sending their boy there. If only similar letters from earlier headmasters had been preserved we should know much more about the early history of the school.

MY LORD,

I am much obliged to you for the favour of your letter which I received this morning. . . . I flatter myself that my plan of education quite corresponds with the sentiments of your friend, being entirely a classical one and to qualify youth for the university, where we have several exhibitions. I find it indeed necessary to have a French master in the house, and a dancing master attends the school from London once a week to teach those whose parents wish them to learn. Boys in general who are intended for trade go from me to some academy about 13 or 14 years of age. There is a very good writing master in the town greatly under my own direction who attends my school every day after classical hours (which are eight every day except holy days) are over.

I have sent the expenses of education here that your friend may be satisfied in every particular. We have no vacation at Easter except from Good Friday to Easter Tuesday and break up only twice a year, at Christmas and Whitsuntide if it falls late; but if soon, as this year, we do not break up till a little before midsummer, to divide the year as equally as possible.

The statement of fees enclosed with the letter runs as follows:

	£	s.	d.	
Entrance	3	3	0	
Board and classical learning	20	0	0	per an.
French if learnt	2	2	0	,,
Writing and accounts	1	4	9	,,
Dancing if learnt	2	15	0	
Latin usher at Xmas		10	6	
Servants ,, ,,		10	6	

From which one gathers that the usher received an inadequate salary from the Governors, and that it was supplemented by a sort of compulsory Christmas box from each parent.

Such, so far as we can now discern it, was Tonbridge School twenty years before the French Revolution.

III. THE KNOXES (1772-1843)

On the death of Mr. Towers the Governors appointed Vicesimus Knox (1772-8) as headmaster, and thereafter they chose as his successors his son Vicesimus (1778-1812) and his grandson Thomas (1812-43). This hereditary succession for three generations must be rare, if not unique, in the annals of the public schools. The name Vicesimus suggests that its holders were junior members of very large families, but this was not so. It was or had become a family name with no numerical significance. Vicesimus II was his father's eldest son, and he too had an eldest son of that name who went to the bar, leaving the succession in Tonbridge to his younger brother. The long tenure of the headmastership by this family was commemorated by 'Knox Lane', formerly the name of the narrow road which runs along the south side of the school property, now called Lansdowne Road. Until very recent times the name 'Lansdowne Road' was to be seen on the south side of the roadway and 'Knox Lane' on the north side of it.

Of Knox I there is but little to be said. Before his appointment to Tonbridge he had been an assistant master at Merchant Taylors', and, as his grandson tells us, 'in addition to the fatigues of his school laboured assiduously in the church', as a curate at St. Dunstans-in-the-East. He seems to have come to Tonbridge a tired man, and the school failed to flourish. Numbers fell to seventeen, a low record only surpassed, so far as we know, by Tommy Roots. There were only eight boarders and three of them were brothers, named Smith. One of these three was afterwards the celebrated Sir Sidney Smith who repulsed Napoleon at Acre in 1799. His school career was not a long one, for he entered the navy at the age of thirteen, but it is recorded that in long after years he visited the place and secured for the boys an extra half holiday.

Vicesimus Knox the Second was a very different man. Though only twenty-six at the time of his appointment he had already achieved some fame as an author. We are told that, having completed a sufficient number of 'Essays, Moral and Literary' to make a volume, he sent his manuscript to a publisher, to publish or destroy them as he thought best. The publisher sent them for an 'opinion' to Dr. Samuel Johnson, then near the end of his life and at the height of his fame. Johnson reported in terms of the highest praise, predicting the future fame of the author. The book proved a popular success with the serious public to which it was addressed. An 1815 reprint (in the school library) is described as 'seventeenth edition'. Among his later works, written during his long headmastership, were *Winter Evenings, or Lucubrations on Life and Letters, Personal Nobility, being Letters addressed to a Young Nobleman*, and *Liberal Education*, a treatise upholding the classical system. In 1824, three years after Knox's death, a dignified seven-volume edition of his *Collected Works* was published. Nobody reads Knox to-day, but his essays and lucubrations are not so very different in tone and quality from the *Idlers* and *Ramblers* of Dr. Johnson.

Under this vigorous and intelligent young man the school moved forward once again towards prosperity, and numbers rose to eighty-five. The headmaster married and was able to live in fine style. An old boy writing to his father, also an old boy, in 1781, says 'Mr. Knox of Tunbridge has a new coach just come out spick and span with a pair of long-tail greys. Is not this quite the thing? My aunt says "Lor' sir, a schoolmaster's is a vastly fine trade" ' (*A History of the Woodgates*, p. 274).

But unhappily the prosperity of Knox's early years was not

to be maintained, and the cause of the decline was the French Revolution. Dr. Knox—an honorary degree had been conferred on him by the University of Philadelphia—was a disciple of Charles James Fox and a fervent apostle of what were called popular liberties. When the Revolution broke out in 1789 his enthusiasm for liberty, equality and fraternity led him to publish several pamphlets in support of the Revolutionists which provoked grave disapprobation among the kind of people that were sending their sons to Tonbridge school. Numbers dropped as quickly as they had risen and in 1793, the year of the outbreak of war between Great Britain and France and of the Reign of Terror, there were only twenty-eight boys in the school.

But this seemed to make no difference to the headmaster: he was prepared to sacrifice the school to his principles. Very noble, no doubt; but it would surely have been nobler still if he had sacrificed himself instead, and resigned his headmastership. Even the outbreak of the war did not change his sympathies any more than they changed those of his leader, Fox, whose party in the House of Commons dwindled till it could all travel in two hackney coaches.

In 1793 Knox and his family spent the summer holidays at Brighton, the first of the new seaside resorts whose 'waters' were in the coming century to prove more popular than those of the old 'watering places' with their supposedly medicinal mineral springs, such as Bath and Tunbridge Wells. As ill luck would have it, he was invited by the vicar to preach at the church of St. Nicholas, and one imagines that for Dr. Knox the preaching of sermons was as much a pleasure as a duty even in his summer holidays. There was a large camp of militia on the outskirts of the town (mentioned in one of Jane Austen's novels) and the town was full of officers and their wives. He took as his text 'Glory to God in the highest; on earth peace and goodwill towards men'.

'I was led', he wrote afterwards in his account of what followed, 'to the choice of this subject from observing the extreme bitterness, even in gay and good-humoured companies, against

38

a great part of our fellow-creatures: from the almost daily accounts in the newspapers of slaughtered thousands and the eagerness with which war had been adopted by all the nations concerned, when negotiations might have effected every desirable purpose, without expense and without carnage.'

'As he developed his theme', says a modern writer on the history of *Brighton*,[1] 'whispers arose among the congregation, "Will the fellow never have done?" Nervous titters sounded out and fans played, as the doctor afterwards expressed it, with motions as rapid as the tail of an angry cat. He was allowed, however, to finish his sermon without interruption and not until he visited the playhouse two days later to see a performance of "An Agreeable Surprise" did he realize what deep offence he had given.'

It was indeed a surprise and not an agreeable one that awaited the doctor. It is related in the *Gentleman's Magazine* for August 1793, 'Last night Dr. Knox and his family were in one of the boxes at the theatre: there were also several officers in the house. At the end of the play a note was handed to Dr. Knox by the box-keeper stating that it was the desire of several gentlemen then present that he should withdraw. The note had no signature, and Dr. Knox took no notice of it. Several officers then stood up and insisted on his leaving the house immediately. A scene of much confusion ensued in which Dr. Knox endeavoured to address himself to the company; he said his sermon had been misunderstood—that he did not mean to convey any reflections upon the constitution of the country, or to speak disrespectfully of the army in general or of any individual in particular belonging to it. The tumult however still continued and Dr. Knox was compelled to leave the house.'

The only difficulty in this account is the statement that the note was presented at the end of the play when one would suppose that both Knox and everyone else would be ready to leave in any case. Perhaps the note was presented during an interval between the acts.

We have wandered away from Tonbridge school, and we

[1] *Brighton*, by Osbert Sitwell and D. Barton, pp. 185–6.

only wish we could immediately return to it. How interesting it would be to study the repercussions of this incident on the masters (if there was more than one assistant) and the boys at the beginning of the autumn term. But no record survives. The Governors, too, must have shaken their heads, but they have left no written record of their forebodings.

Dr. Knox was not, of course, always so unfortunate with his sermons. *The Times* of 3rd September 1802 reports that his sermon at Margate in aid of the Infirmary 'drew tears from the whole congregation'. People wept more easily in those days; we often hear of tears being shed in the House of Commons.

We know very little of the remaining twenty-nine years of the headmastership of this, the second, Vicesimus Knox. Numbers rose to forty-one in the year of his retirement. The lists for most of the intervening years are lost, but it seems unlikely that the school ever recovered the prosperity of the ten years preceding the Revolution. However, the doctor was venerated by his pupils and many of them achieved a respectable distinction in after life. One of them, a French boy, le Comte Pierre Dumoustier, became a general under Napoleon, and took occasion during the brief truce of the Treaty of Amiens to visit England and call upon his old headmaster.

Dr. Knox is the earliest headmaster of whom we have a portrait. He was described as 'about middle height, his countenance dark and his eye thoughtful and expressive'.

In 1782 Edward Hasted published the second volume of his *History of Kent*. It contains an account of Skinners' Day, worth comparing in its details with the order of events as we know them to-day. The school, he says, 'continues under the management of the Company of Skinners who in pursuance of the statutes visit it annually in the month of May at very considerable expense. They are attended, as the statutes direct, by a very respectable clergyman of London whose business it is to examine the several classes of the school. On the arrival of the Company, etc., in their carriages at the gates of the school a congratulatory oration in Latin is spoken by the head boy. The Company then proceed to church where they distribute bread money and cloaths to a number of poor persons of the parishes of Tonbridge, Bidborough and Speldhurst according to the will of Sir Thomas Smythe. On their return, after a cold collation, they survey the buildings and give orders for all necessary repairs. They next proceed to the school where, after a few Latin orations, the examination begins; at the close of which the whole company, which consists, besides the visitors and their friends, of the neighbouring gentry and clergy, retire to dinner which is served up in the library (i.e. the headmaster's dining-room) and in other rooms in the headmaster's house. At five o'clock they return to the school and the grammatical disputations, a very ancient exercise, are commenced by the six senior scholars. These exercises conclude with the repetition of English or Latin verses. The examiner then distributes, according to the statutes, as honorary reward, a silver pen gilt to each of the six senior scholars who on that day walk in procession to the church before their patrons, with garlands of fresh flowers on their heads. Such is the form which has been constantly observed since the foundation of the school.'

Perhaps the six pens mentioned in this account should be three. Anyhow there were three in Sir Andrew Judd's statutes, and there are three to-day. Hasted does not mention the curious custom of decorating the school and the High Street with sprigs of birch on Skinners' Day. No one seems to know the origin or significance of this custom, though, to be sure, the birch is a tree traditionally associated with education.

Thomas Knox (1812-43) succeeded his father Vicesimus[1] in the year of Napoleon's Russian campaign. Waterloo followed three years later, and peace brought the usual post-war slump. In those days banks were small local affairs with none of the capacity to survive bad times possessed by the 'big five' of to-day. The Tonbridge bank went bankrupt, bringing down many of the leading families of the neighbourhood whose sons

---

[1] Before we leave this gentleman we might speculate as to how he pronounced his Christian name. Certainly not Wee-kaysimus, which is the modern class-room orthodoxy. It must have been either Vi-sessimus or Vi-seesimus, probably the latter.

had for generations been educated at the school, the Woodgates of Summerhill for example and the Childrens of Ferox Hall.[1] Numbers were once again under thirty.

However a change was impending which was going to open up new prospects for the school. In 1806 a long lease granted to the Duke of Bedford of the land in the parish of St. Pancras, which the Founder had acquired as part of the endowment of the school, came to an end. London was spreading out northwards, as the names of Regents Park and Regent Street, called after the Prince Regent (1811-20) remind us. James Burton, the great speculative builder of the time took building leases of Sir Andrew Judd's pastureland in 1807 and the income produced by the property increased from a few pounds to over £4,000 a year.

The question now arose, to whom did this income belong? Did it belong to the school, for which the Skinners' Company were trustees, or did it belong to the Skinners' Company, to be used by them at their own discretion after they had fulfilled their modest statutory duties towards the school? The story is a tangled one, and for those who dislike such stories, dry; but it had better be told.

The Founder had, during his lifetime, arranged the conveyance of this land to himself and his servant, Henry Fisher, for the purposes of the school, and Fisher had, after his death, conveyed it for the same purpose to the Skinners' Company. But for some reason unknown Judd had not been content to let the matter rest there but, by his will, had devised the property all over again to the Skinners' Company in terms similar to but not identical with the trusts of the conveyance. In the course of the subsequent litigation between the Skinners and Andrew Fisher, already mentioned in the first chapter of this book, the title of the Skinners' Company to the property on behalf of the school had been confirmed by Acts of Parliament passed in 1572 and 1589. The question of the ownership of the property depended on the true effect of all these docu-

[1] Both these families, though no longer in occupation of the houses mentioned above, have sent boys to the school in very recent years.

ments. The Skinners claimed that it belonged to them; the people of Tonbridge contended through their representatives that it belonged to the school; the headmaster and usher whose regular wages, though supplemented by gratuities from the Company and the fluctuating profits of their boarding houses, were still only thirty pounds and twelve pounds a year respectively, thought they were entitled to a share of the spoil; and each of the parties could point to words in one or other of the documents in support of their claim.

This was the position when, in 1813, Parliament passed an Act appointing commissioners to inquire into educational endowments, to investigate all breaches of trust therein, and to report thereon. Strictly speaking, 'free schools' which had governors appointed by their Founder were excluded from the scope of the inquiry, but this proviso of the Act seems to have been ignored by all parties, so far as Tonbridge school was concerned. We do not know whether the commissioners took the initiative in ignoring this provision of the Act, or whether they were called upon to include Tonbridge in their inquiry by one of the interested parties. In either case they took evidence from the Company and the headmaster, and reported. After describing the circumstances of the school they add the words: 'How far the Company of Skinners are right in treating the surplus (of the endowment income) after paying these salaries (i.e. £30 to the headmaster and £12 to the usher) and repairs as their own is a question which can only be solved by judicial decision'.

Thereupon a Bill was filed in the Court of Chancery in the name of the Attorney-General against the Skinners' Company and their clerk, claiming an account of all the land and property conveyed to the Company by the Founder or his trustees and a declaration that all the rents and profits thereof ought to be applied to the support of the school. The proceedings were undertaken at the instance of the vicar of Tonbridge and three citizens of the town, their solicitor being William Scoones, O.T., a Tonbridge lawyer. There seems, however, no doubt that the headmaster was the moving spirit in setting the law in

43

motion. The case on behalf of the school, which was conducted separately from that of the town was argued by Anthony Hart, O.T., the leader of the Chancery bar, afterwards raised to the peerage as Vice-Chancellor of England.

We need not examine the arguments advanced on either side. The verdict was given in favour of the school, to which henceforth the whole endowment belonged. This necessitated a new scheme which in 1825 superseded Sir Andrew Judd's original charter. The number of boarders that might be taken by the headmaster was raised from twelve to sixty, the number to be taken by the usher or second master from eight to forty. Any assistant master might take twenty boys, and any housekeeper in Tonbridge licensed by the Governors might take thirty boys. Here were preparations for a large school, which did not for a long time materialize.

Secondly the headmaster's salary was raised to £500 and that of the usher to £200.

The privileges of free education apart from extras (which included all subjects except classics) were extended to all boys whose parents or guardians resided within ten miles by road of Tonbridge church. These were to be called foundationers. Non-foundationers were to pay an annual fee of ten guineas. It may be said that this distinction still persists, in that foundationers still receive an annual deduction of ten pounds on their tuition fees. Of course nearly all foundationers are day boys and non-foundationers boarders, but there are usually one or two day boys who travel in by train or bus from outside the ten-mile limit, and a rather larger number of boarders whose parents live within the limit and thus secure the foundationers' privilege. The ten miles is now calculated 'as the crow flies' by a circle drawn on an ordnance map with Tonbridge church as its centre.

Sixteen new exhibitions of £100 a year were created for boys proceeding to Oxford and Cambridge, tenable for four years, and foundationers were to be preferred to non-foundationers in the award of these exhibitions. This last proved a most mistaken provision, for it came to mean that any dunce capable of passing the entrance examinations of the universities might claim preference over a first-rate scholar who happened to be a non-foundationer. This state of affairs was, after an agitation dating at least from the establishment of the *Tonbridgian* (1858) if not earlier, ended by the constitution granted to the school by the Charity Commissioners in 1880. Since that date the exhibitions have been open to all competitors.

The exhibitions were to be awarded at the annual visitation of the Skinners' Company, which was shifted from May to the end of the summer term, after an examination conducted by an examiner appointed by All Souls College, Oxford.

The report of the educational endowment commission which set in motion the course of events just described contains a valuable description of the school as it stood in 1819: 'The number of boys strictly on the foundation is ten, who are all day scholars, which Mr. Knox states to be about the average of the last sixty years. . . . The master is allowed by the statutes to receive boarders . . . he has at present about thirty boarders. . . . Dr. Thomas Knox stated in his evidence: "The present boys on the foundation are the sons of gentlemen in the neighbourhood and respectable tradesmen. . . . The foundation boys receive a classical education in Latin and Greek, and, if required, Hebrew. This is all the instruction that I consider them to be entitled to under the foundation: but they are also taught English, reading, writing, arithmetic, and the various branches of mathematics, at the charge of one guinea a quarter. The foundation boys are taught with the boarders; I make no distinction whatever, either in or out of the school hours, but encourage them to mix together.'

With prospects of the school thus enlarged by the award of the Court of Chancery and the 1825 scheme the Governors set about enlarging the school premises. At that date the school playing field extended from the back of the school building, which was close to the roadway, as far as the end of what is now the gravel parade ground. The Governors in 1825 purchased from Thomas Martin what is now known as 'the Head' and the mainly unused small ground to the north of it. These were once doubtless called 'Martins', though the name has long since got transferred to the field further west, purchased at a much later date. The well-known iron posts, dated 1826, marked the limit of this purchase, though most of them have been moved from their original positions.

At about the same time the Governors purchased the Georgian house now known as Old Judde, to be a boarding house for the second master or usher. Thus originated the oldest of the regular boarding houses other than School House. Judde House moved to its present quarters in 1893, and 'Old Judde' thenceforth served a variety of purposes till it was provided with an entirely new 'inside' as up-to-date classrooms in 1926.

In fact for many years to come all these ambitious preparations for a golden future must have seemed a trifle premature and perhaps miscalculated. The banquet was prepared, but the guests did not arrive. *Deus dat incrementum*, says the school motto. Providence, ordaining the growth of London, had increased the endowment, but where was the increase in that primary necessity of boys' schools—namely, boys? At first all went well and in 1827 there were over a hundred boys in the school for the first time in its history. But decline soon set in again and when Thomas Knox retired in 1843 there were only fifty-five boys. And it is worth remarking that, if one allows for the great increase in the country's population during the previous fifty years, fifty-five boys represented relatively a much smaller school than the same numbers had implied under Cawthorn a hundred years before.

The cause of the trouble may have been, once again, the political enthusiasms of the Knox family. Just as the French Revolution had proved a fatal bait to the leftward appetites of Vicesimus, so did the Reform Bill agitation of 1830-2 to his son Thomas. The so-called Great Reform Bill, which abolished the rotten boroughs but only added one quarter of a million persons to the electorate, seems to us to-day a measure at once obvious and unenterprising, but it roused more lively ardours and apprehensions than any other purely political issue between

46

the deposition of James II and the present day. And rightly so; for behind the typically English moderation of the proposals was the fundamental issue: is democracy the goal of the future or a poison-plant to be nipped in the bud? That had also been the issue underlying the French Revolution, as Burke had indicated. Both the Knoxes took what was in the end to prove the winning side, but it was not the side supported by the kind of people who might be thinking of sending their boys to Tonbridge. Thomas Arnold of Rugby, whose headmastership coincides with the latter half of Thomas Knox's reign, was no doubt also an advanced Liberal, and founded at Rugby a long-lived Liberal tradition on which the school flourished exceedingly. But Thomas of Rugby was a great man, and Thomas of Tonbridge was not. In any case it seems to have been the general opinion that the decline of the school numbers after 1830 was due to Knox's political activities, and more particularly to a speech he delivered at Penenden Heath near Maidstone during the time of serious rioting that preceded the final passage of the Bill through the House of Lords.

During eleven years of Dr. Knox's headmastership Tonbridge participated in an endowment more than a hundred years older than that of Sir Andrew Judde. In 1442 John Carpenter, the executor of Sir Richard Whittington,[1] the richest London merchant of his day, made a bequest of property in London to pay for the education of four poor boys. Early in the nineteenth century the Carpenter property, like the Judd property, had risen in value and it was felt that more money should be spent on the 'Carpenter scholars' than the twenty pounds per annum hitherto allowed. They were, in 1826, sent to Tonbridge, their fees being paid from the Carpenter foundation. Dr. Knox was not favourably impressed. 'A boy', he writes, 'has been sent by the present Lord Mayor—totally unfit to enter the school—his manners low and vulgar—his ignorance

---

[1] This is 'Dick Whittington' whom an Elizabethan dramatist provided with a cat and an entirely unhistorical legend, thus equipping him for his modern immortality as a pantomime hero. It is as though, in the twenty-fifth century, the present Lord Nuffield were to be represented on the Christmas stage by a 'principal boy' in tights.

extreme—his faculties, I suspect imperfect. . . . It is extraordinary that out of four boys two should be silly.' In 1837, however, the Carpenter endowment was used for founding the City of London School and the Carpenter scholars were transferred to it.

A pleasant picture of school life near the end of the Knoxian epoch was written in after years by J. F. Wadmore who was a boy in the school at the time. Wadmore was subsequently both a member of the Skinners' Company and an architect. He built the old school chapel, now the library, the cricket pavilion, and the house immediately to the north of the school called Dry Hill House, in which he lived until his death in 1903. It is the house that was, from 1926 onwards the headquarters, first of both the Day Boy Houses, and afterwards of one of them, namely, Smythe House.

'We walked up with my father to see Dr. Knox . . . we found him in his garden and he took us over the school and grounds. Well do I remember his fine and portly figure, his shaggy eyebrows and bright eye, and on my father saying his boys had brought their bats the doctor remarked, "Yes, quite right, quite right: I never knew a boy worth anything who was not fond of cricket. . . ."

'Under the statutes the school should have commenced on a Thursday, but this rule was relaxed, and although my father sent us back on that day the school did not commence until Monday and the majority of the boys returned on Saturday. After the departure of my father to town we had still two days before us, and with the instructions and under the guidance of a schoolboy we went down town and proceeded to purchase knives, plates, spoons, forks, saucepans, tea cups and tea-pots, it being the custom for each boy to find and take care of his own, and to provide himself with tea, coffee and milk, etc., as we were only provided by the doctor with bread and butter and milk for breakfast and tea.

'At dinner-time it was a cheerful sight to see the doctor enter the hall, where the boys were assembled, with his hat on, his black Tommy—a short, knotty holly stick with a grotesque head carved at one end of it and tapering away at the other—under his arm, wearing a silk handkerchief for an apron. He was closely followed by Bert, his butler, more portly than his master . . . and behind him came Killick (school porter, 1826-75) and others with vegetables, etc.

'Occasionally it was his wont to enter the school-room about ten o'clock in the morning or four o'clock on fine afternoons and, having informed the boys that he was well satisfied with the work either of the fifth or sixth forms, take a new cricket ball from his capacious pocket and throw it into the centre of the school as a signal that it was a let-out[1] or a holiday, and with a shout the boys would make for the door and rush out into the field for a game of cricket. In the autumn months hockey was the favourite game. Hockey-cutting on half-holidays was a glorious treat; tramping through the woods and selecting the best formed sticks and cutting them off with a bill; this however was not always practicable as the noise made in cutting the tree frequently called attention to the fact that a trespass was being committed. Then came a "chivey" over the fields and across country; but rarely, if ever, were any boys caught as they always outstripped their enraged pursuers, bringing the sticks off in triumph, which were dried in the chimney of the upper school after being steamed and bent to the required shape.

'There were six monitors who read prayers in turn every morning and evening.

'The work generally in the sixth was Sophocles, Thucydides, Aeschylus, Horace, Virgil. The head boy selected the passages for composition, and the doctor chose the subject for the verses and theme. In the fifth the books used were Herodotus, Cicero, and Horace; in the fourth Sallust, Virgil and a little Anacreon; in the third Greek fables, Cornelius Nepos and Virgil; in the upper second Ovid and Caesar with Greek grammar; in the lower second Latin fables and Eutropius, in both cases Ellis's

---

[1] This term is still, a hundred years later, in regular use at Tonbridge, meaning a postponement of lock-up on Saturday evenings in the summer term. I do not think it is generally used at other schools.

exercises; in the first Latin Grammar and English. . . . In those days a "construe" was generally made to the accompaniment of an impending cane in case of a mistake. Punishment was almost always corporal. The unheard-of punishment of writing out 500 lines of Homer was once given by the doctor who caught a boy, *flagrante delicto*, riding his favourite heifer round the cricket field. The Rev. E. Vinall, who was curate of the parish church . . . taught mathematics to the fifth and sixth forms.

'Previous to 1838 the annual cricket matches played by the school were two only, one against the town and the other against the old boys. Russell was the great slow bowler against the school, and his friend Waite, who always played in top boots, was one of the stoutest and steadiest, if not the most agile, batsman on the side of the town, who used to muster in strong force as spectators. Killick, whose face as school porter (and previously coachman to Dr. Knox) was familiar to every Tonbridge school boy from 1826-75, used to tell how the second eleven ground was the scene of many a rough and hard-fought struggle of old. There was the doctor on horseback, taking a hearty interest in the game; there were the townspeople sitting in groups on the slopes, sucking their pipes and drinking barrels of beer and cider which were placed under the trees that line the south side of the ground. Then at one o'clock the two elevens and the whole school used to adjourn to the dining hall and dine together. The doctor would then call upon one of the opposite eleven, Parker the inn-keeper, or the three Coombers, famous for their glee singing, to give a song. It was one of the merriest days of the year for the school, and no one apparently enjoyed it more than the doctor himself, who not infrequently would sing them "The Brave Old Oak" or "The Old English Gentleman".'

All of which prompts the reflection that, if much has been gained by the progress of the last hundred years, something has also been lost.

Mr. Wadmore does not mention football, but another Old Boy, Albany de Fonblanque, writing of the years immediately following Wadmore's time, mentions football as the game of

the autumn term, and relegates hockey to the Lent term.[1]
Tonbridge had already, like other schools, adopted the three-
term system in place of the two terms a year ordained by the
Founder, and usual until the early years of the nineteenth century. At Eton, I believe, a term is still called a 'half', i.e. a half-
year. Mr. de Fonblanque also tells us that one of the masters
who boarded boys supplied and cooked all their food, and that
this enlightened establishment was on that account somewhat
despised by the boys of the other houses.

In other respects Fonblanque's account strikingly confirms
Wadmore's, both in detail and in general atmosphere; but he
adds something about less approved activities.

'The railway was not completed when I first came (in 1842),
but the whole place teemed with "navvies", and for some reason
every youth of the lower order was known as a navvy and
regarded as a natural foe. We had our little wars with them as
with frontier tribes. There was a frontier tribe in a row of
cottages in the London road to the right of the gate at the end
of the Avenue, and they constantly attacked us—or we them.
A sort of Town and Gown row was chronic. There was an
epoch-making battle between Arthur Sandilands and the
Grand Sachem of all the navvies, whose name I forget, under
the trees right in front of the school gates, in which our cham-
pion prevailed. One winter, when the snow lay thick, the
navvies began the war by harmless snowballing of the day boys
as they came in. After a little they bound up stones in their
snowballs and cut some of us, who were pelting back, badly.
Then we sallied out with hockey-sticks on a punitive expedi-
tion and did well. Then the enemy armed themselves with
similar weapons and illegally barked our knuckles. Then we
called out the fencing-class with their basket-handled single-
sticks, and there was lamentation and woe. The order was,
slice the navvy over the shins and when he stooped to rub
them give him "number one" over the nape of the neck. That

---

[1] A. de Fonblanque entered the School under Dr. Knox and died in 1924,
at the age of ninety-four, during the headmastership of Mr. Sloman. By profession a member of the consular service, he also wrote a number of novels.

settled it. Alas! for these glories of the past: I find that the present generation does not know what "a navvy" means.'

Which may be the sort of thing someone (not the Duke of Wellington) had in mind when he said that the Battle of Waterloo was won on the playing fields of Eton. He was certainly not alluding to decorously organized games, played in accordance with rigid codes of sportsmanship after the manner of to-day; for such things did not exist at the time.

As the present generation does not know what a navvy means, either in Tonbridge slang or in wider usage, we may as well explain. The original navvies were the diggers of canals, employees of the various Internal Navigation Companies. The period between Waterloo and the accession of Victoria was not only the golden age of stage coaches; it was also a time of astonishing activity in canal making and planning. A very interesting map possessed by Mr. Stoneley the builder, whose offices are opposite the school, shows a complete network of canals planned for the county of Kent. Most of them were never made, for the railways superseded the canals as they superseded the stage-coaches and the arterial road-making which gave us, for example, the magnificent design of Pol Hill. An interesting example of one of these canals, half dug and never finished, is to be found just south of the weir and the Redhill railway, about two miles west of Tonbridge. The term navvy was transferred from the canal diggers to the men who dug the cuttings and built the embankments of the railways. The line which came to Tonbridge at this time was not the direct line to London with its numerous and costly tunnels—that came twenty-five years later—but the original London-Dover line, branching off the London-Brighton line by a right-angle turn at Redhill.

Dr. Knox turned the railway building to good use. He bought earth excavated from the cuttings and used it for levelling 'the Head'. The event was commemorated by a brass plate let into the stump of a tree at the south-east corner of the ground. The original plate has long been lost, but a copy of the inscription is still to be seen on the wall of the pavilion. 'Hanc aream aequandam curavit Thomas Knox S.T.P. huius scholae magister A.D. 1838'—which may have helped the boys to master the gerundive construction.[1]

In the time of the Knoxes the day before Skinners' Day used to be called 'Flowering Day', for the senior boys collected flowers from the gardens of friends of the school to decorate the school and to provide the garlands which the three pen-winners were to wear on Skinners' Day. These adornments were not garlands in the usual sense but were worn on the head as caps. Dr. Thomas Knox used to give a ball on the evening of Skinners' Day and the garlanded trio were privileged to select their partners and lead off the opening dance.

'The doctor' died suddenly of heart-failure near the end of the summer term of 1843. He was, as we have shown, a genial and agreeable man, and he was capable, at times, of rather schoolmasterly jokes. A boy named Taswell once arrived late for tea. 'Well, Taswell', said the doctor, 'as you are so late you would be *as well* without your *T*.' Rather heartless perhaps, but justified on the same ground as bear-baiting, according to the classic defence—that it gave more pleasure to the spectators than it gave pain to the bear.

With the passing of the third Knox we reach the end of the 'ancient history' of the pre-Victorian 'free grammar school', for under his successor the school was to expand to the dimensions of what we now reckon a public school. Only one thing need be said in retrospection of the period of 290 years that we have covered, and it is this. It is commonly assumed that the school of those old days was not only much smaller than the school of modern times, but that it catered for a humbler class of person. School lists are only available at certain dates, and even when they are available many of the names convey no certain information. But the researches of Mr. W. G. Hart, embodied in his *Old Tonbridge School Lists* show that at certain times if not at all times the school contained a number of boys from the families of the landed gentry, the 'county families' as we say. We do not assert this fact for the school's credit. Kind

---

[1] S.T.P.—sanctae theologiae professor—is Latin for D.D., Doctor of Divinity.

hearts, no doubt, are more than coronets. Coronets may be deplorable and disgusting objects. But they indubitably exist, and Tonbridge school was more frequented, at some early periods, by the offspring of baronets and such-like persons than it is to-day, when county families go further afield and from all over England congregate at Eton. The old grammar schools were less class-bound establishments than the modern public schools. John Hampden of Hampden rubbed shoulders at Thame Grammar School with the local farmers' sons, and so it was, no doubt, with the embryo baronets who received their education at Tonbridge.

IV. DR. WELLDON (1843-75)

In 1842, the year before the death of Thomas Knox, occurred two events of great symbolical importance, the opening of Tonbridge railway station and the death of Arnold of Rugby.

The building of the main line railways, which fell within the first ten years of Victoria's reign, was important for the public schools in two ways. In the first place, it was one of the main causes of the great Victorian prosperity, which enormously increased the numbers of the class that could afford a boarding-school education for their sons. (The other main causes, if one may dogmatize on so intricate a subject, were the establishment of free trade and the opening of the new gold fields in California and Australia.) In the second place it enlarged, if one may so express it, the geographical outlook of these people. Hitherto most of them had thought in terms of a radius of perhaps fifty miles. I have read somewhere (though I cannot lay my finger on the authority) that in one of Dr. Arnold's sixth forms not a single boy had seen the sea. Rugby is situated almost exactly in the middle of England; consequently its boys were Midlanders, and the sea was outside the geographical movements of their families. But with the railways anyone could go anywhere in England in a few hours and at trifling expense. Henceforth a successful school could draw its boys from all over the country.

The railways and the new prosperity, therefore, created a new opportunity for boarding schools. But the question was, would they succeed in taking it? Would the newly enriched middle classes want what these schools had to offer? That is where the importance of Arnold comes in. The newly enriched middle classes were sober, serious folk, very conscious of their own virtues and by no means anxious to follow, in all respects, the manners and customs of the gentry. The typical public schools of the Waterloo epoch, the Eton of Dr. Keate or the Harrow of Dr. George Butler, nurseries of scholarship and statesmanship, no doubt, but notorious for every kind of dare-devilry, were not at all what the new middle class wanted. It was Arnold who, in the words of G. M. Young,[1] 'reconciled the serious classes to the public school'. A radical thinker by the standards of his day, but also a man of overwhelming religious earnestness, he made the chapel the centre of school life, and left the impress of his earnestness on a high percentage of his pupils. An authority on Greek history, he saw his school not merely as a place where boys came to learn lessons, but as a miniature community, like the city states of ancient Greece, where the lessons of citizenship were to be learnt through self-government. 'The sixth' learnt to govern the school, and 'the sixth' were Arnold's disciples.

Modern writers have pointed out that Arnold was less of an innovator than is commonly supposed. Indeed Arnold himself used to say that most of what he did at Rugby was what he had himself seen in practice when a boy at Winchester. But this is unimportant. What Arnold contributed was not this idea or that but his own dominating personality. He drew the attention of the public as no headmaster had done before. Perhaps his success was in part posthumous, and due to one of his pupils. It is not often that a novel influences opinion, but *Tom Brown's Schooldays*, published in 1857, introduced to thousands of readers a new idea of what school might be. They felt that such an education for their sons was worth the sacrifice of home ties and of a considerable sum of money.

Henceforth some, though not all, of the scores of little grammar schools were destined to expand with astonishing

---

[1] *Victorian England*, by G. M. Young, p. 97.

2. A VIEW OF THE GRAMMAR SCHOOL AT TONBRIDGE IN KENT

from a picture painted and presented to the Worshipful Company of Skinners, London, by Jonah Smith Wells, jun., Master 1831

3. THE STAFF 1863

NAMES (LEFT TO RIGHT): SEATED: *Rev. E. I. Welldon, Dr. J. I. Welldon, Rev. J. Stroud, Rev. D. S. Ingram;* STANDING: *J. Berncastel,* (unknown), *E. H. Goggs, Rev. J. Langhorne, D. Hanbury, J. W. Little, W. E. McGill*

rapidity into schools on the national scale, numbering their boys not by dozens but by hundreds. Which schools would catch the favourable tide? There might be two little grammar schools within a few miles of one another, Oakham and Uppingham in the Midlands, Sevenoaks and Tonbridge in Kent. Why did the latter of each of these pairs go ahead and leave the former behind?—because it was the first to secure a successful headmaster. Uppingham had Thring. Welldon was not a man of Thring's calibre or originality, but he was a sound and attractive man, and he served the purpose.

James Ind Welldon was a man of thirty-two when he became headmaster, but he had already served for seven years as second master at Shrewsbury, first under Butler and afterwards under Kennedy (author of the famous Latin Primer), two headmasters who between them raised Shrewsbury to a position not far behind Rugby among the progressive boarding schools. He started with only 43 boys, but numbers rose rapidly from the first, reaching 107 in 1844, 163 in 1858 and 235 when he left in 1875. Though he reigned thirty-two years his is, so far as we can make out, the first long reign which had not ended with a decline. 235 may seem a modest number, but in proportion to the total public school population of the country it probably counted for as much as 470, the official maximum (sometimes exceeded) of recent years, counted for in the 1930's.

To this great increase day boys contributed as well as boarders. In 1867, to take one of the years for which an exact division into the two elements is possible, there were 94 boarders and 73 day boys. Since the coming of the railway Tonbridge town had been growing almost as fast as Tonbridge school.

The increase in numbers clearly called for additional classrooms and dormitories, but even more important for the welfare of the school in the headmaster's estimation was the building of a school chapel. This was not, as has been sometimes assumed, because the school was becoming inconveniently big for accommodation in the parish church; indeed for many years after the building of the chapel the school continued to attend the parish church on Sunday mornings in accordance with the Founder's statutes. It was because, according to the new ideas associated with Dr. Arnold of Rugby, a school chapel was the most important of all possible instruments of real education, which was not the learning of lessons or the playing of games but the formation of character.

Dr. Welldon approached the Governors on the subject of a school chapel in 1848 but found them unsympathetic. They said they had no funds available for the purpose and did not appreciate the need for it. Ten years later, however, the Governors consented to the building of a chapel provided that the endowment was not called on for the cost of it. A subscription list was therefore opened, to which many of the Governors individually contributed, and a fund of £2,500 was raised. Things seem to have moved quickly, for not only was the foundation stone laid in 1859 but the chapel was opened by Dr. Sumner, Archbishop of Canterbury, in the same year.[1] The chapel was intended, we are told, to hold 200 people. It must, one supposes, have held many more, when the number of the boys alone rose considerably above 200, but perhaps the day boys did not attend the chapel services. With singular forethought Dr. Welldon did not have the chapel formally consecrated. He foresaw that the school would outgrow it, and that the building would then be put to secular uses. One of its stained-glass windows, an incongruous though interesting memorial of the past, still remains in its west end. There is a tradition, baseless perhaps, that it is to remain there until the last of those who worshipped in the old chapel has died. The building ceased to be used as a chapel in 1892.

Before going further we should chronicle the earliest and undoubtedly the most beautiful of Dr. Welldon's contributions to the school estate, namely the planting, in 1845, of the chestnut avenue.

---

[1] Sumner is said to have been the last Anglican bishop to officiate in a wig. In the eighteenth century all respectable persons wore wigs. Bishops continued to wear them, as a professional distinction, some time longer. Lawyers have not yet discarded them, and perhaps never will.

The problem of secular accommodation was becoming acute, but all the Governors could afford at the moment (1858) was the erection of a wooden hut containing three class-rooms along the side of the playground—now 'the Square' where the corps parades; it had been converted from grass to gravel when Knox bought 'the Head'. However, a very few years later a stroke of luck befell the school. The Midland Railway, originally a network of lines in the Midlands, was building an extension to London and the youngest of the great London termini, St. Pancras, was about to be built. The land required for the goods yard adjoining St. Pancras Station was part of the Sandhills estate of Sir Andrew Judd's bequest, and the railway company acquired compulsory powers to buy this land at a handsome price from the Skinners' Company. Thus the Governors found themselves possessed of a substantial sum in cash for the service of the school and the result was the building, in 1863, of the southern half of the present main school building, stretching from the headmaster's house to the arch, and comprising school house dormitories (now 'cubies'), class-rooms, and the place of assembly for lectures and suchlike purposes called Big School, a name since transferred to its successor. In or under the foundation stone of this building were deposited, according to custom, contemporary coins, newspapers and photographs. Among the photographs was a group of the staff including E. H. Goggs, who lived on as a bachelor in Tonbridge till 1931. I remember in quite recent years the old man striking the foundation stone with his stick and telling me that his photograph was inside it.

At the same time, 'without regret', says the current issue of the *Tonbridgian* (of which more anon), the old Elizabethan school, built while Sir Andrew Judde was still alive, was demolished. To-day all thoughtful persons must regret that act of vandalism very much indeed. No doubt the interior of the building, as it then was, deserved all the hard things said about it. But the interior could have been entirely removed and replaced with whatever the new circumstances required (as was done with 'Old Judde' in 1927). If the old building had been preserved, not only should we still possess an object of beauty and historic interest, visibly connecting the present day school with its origins; we should also have a quadrangle, screened from the publicity and to some extent from the noise of the High Street. But it is useless to repent of the sins of other people, and we are not likely to repeat the offence for, sad to say, we have nothing of equal value to destroy. There are, of course, old parts in School House, though the building as a whole would puzzle an architectural analyst; Old Judde, since the removal of the ugly additions made when it was a boarding house, has been restored to something like its original Georgian form, and there is much that is old and fine in the private sides of Ferox Hall and Manor House. But these three last only came within the school in the nineteenth century. They were not born with it and built for it.

The new building, with the wooden class-rooms, provided accommodation for teaching and increased living space for the boarders of School House. Other boarders were accommodated in Old Judde, which had been opened as the Second Master's house under Thomas Knox. In 1855 Judde House was taken over by the Rev. Edward Ind Welldon, brother of the headmaster, who had joined the staff in 1844. He died in 1879 and was the last of the old 'second masters', with a salary and constitutional position distinct from and superior to the mere assistant masters. In 1867 Park House, the first of the houses outside the school grounds was opened, under the Rev. J. R. Little. He passed the house on in 1890 to H. R. Stokoe who ruled it for forty-one years and in his later years had often the pleasure of guiding the footsteps of the sons of his own old boys.

In 1858, the school magazine, the *Tonbridgian*, was started and has continued without a break ever since. Other schools produced magazines at much earlier dates, but they proved ephemeral. It has been asserted, and is very likely true, that the *Tonbridgian* has had a longer continuous existence than any other school magazine. For some years the finance of the venture was precarious but Dr. Welldon, 'on the strong representations of one of its editors', made the purchase of the paper compulsory for boarders,[1] and in modern times its profits have made a small but steady contribution to the Amalgamated Fund which supports all kinds of activities, mainly athletic. The editor whose 'strong representations' we have mentioned was Septimus Rivington, one of the most actively loyal of the Old Boys of the school. Only five years after leaving, in 1869, he published the first full-length history of the school, and lived to supervise a fourth and greatly enlarged edition of his work, brought up to date in 1925.

The appearance of the *Tonbridgian* is a less important event, no doubt, than the building of the chapel and the new school building, but for the historian its value is unique. All at once the school comes to life, in the eye of posterity, as a social microcosm. For every single term we have vivid, authoritative and delightfully miscellaneous contemporary documents. It is no exaggeration to say that henceforth there is more documentary matter available for each single year of the school's internal activities than for the whole of the previous three hundred years of the school's existence. We make no excuse for quoting freely from this source.[2] And let us begin with football.

Football is one of the oldest because one of the most natural of games and can be traced back to the middle ages, but there were either no rules or every locality played in its own way. There was, for example, a kind of cross-country football with goals in different parishes. Readers of *Tom Brown*, which describes the Rugby of Arnold in the 'thirties', will remember that in the match between School House and the rest of the school, *all* the boys played, the lesser lights being assembled in a solid array to defend their own goal. We have an account of

[1] 'Why not day boys also?' one may well ask. But such curious distinctions long survived. As late as 1932 the purchase of the terminal School Calendar, long compulsory for boarders, was voluntary for day boys.

[2] The School Library possesses two sets of *Tonbridgians*. The 'red' set, which is on the open shelves of the Library, has several gaps, mostly in the period 1870–95. The 'brown' set, which is absolutely complete, is rightly kept under lock and key by the Librarian, to whom any student who requires an issue which happens to be missing from the 'red' set, can apply.

Tonbridge football in Welldon's first years, twelve years or so before the *Tonbridgian* started, from the pen of Albany de Fonblanque.

'We played football on the gravel playground, thereby encouraging several respectable trades including that of the sticking-plaster maker, and enjoyed "the glory and the gutter" in substantial form. The old playground was bounded on the right, looking towards the "head", by the fenced-off garden of Brown's (i.e. of Old Judde; Brown was second master before Edward Welldon) and on the left by a lane which ran parallel to the wall of the headmaster's garden, and leading to the stable yard, divided from our territory by a picket fence. Along the fences on either side was a stone gutter, and when at hockey or at football the leather got into this there was a rush, a lawless scrummage, and a good deal of very lively shinning. In the fence along the lane were several gaps known as "hospitals" because, after a gutter, players were apt to sit in them to examine and nurse their damaged shins. Our hockey and football were played in primitive style—two unorganized mobs hitting, or kicking, up and down towards the goals, represented by the gates leading into the "head" and the London road respectively. We had only one rule that I remember, and that corresponded to the "offside" of this more scientific age. The kick-off was from goal and then the sides charged each other like South African Impis'—i.e. Zulu or Matabele war bands: Fonblanque must have written at a date when these were in the topical newspaper vocabulary.

Now to pass on to the *Tonbridgian* of 1858. 'At the beginning of football there is a good deal of spirit in the games but after a month or so interest lags. Now this occurs to a much less extent at other schools; and the reason, I take it, is this; at other schools they have divisions at football, corresponding to our elevens at cricket, and, consequently, the players feel a noble desire to be one of the "twenty" or whatever the number may be. I suggest, therefore, that this school should have divisions or classes in football as well as in cricket; and that as the school consists of almost exactly 170, I suggest that a

"twenty", a "fifty", and a "hundred" would be the best numbers'—which means presumably a best game playing ten-a-
side, a second game playing twenty-five a side, etc. What
exactly came of this is not clear, but something must have come
of it, for the football match ground off the Shipbourne road
still bears the name of 'the Fifty', and the small ground above
the Head is, or quite recently was, called 'the Upper Hundred'. 'The Fifty' was not used by the school till after Welldon's time, but the name was doubtless transferred to it from
the ground where the original 'fifty' played.

Pass on to 1859 and we find a new set of rules for the Tonbridge game introduced, as follows: (i) No player is to 'pass on'
the ball, in the air or otherwise; (ii) no player is to hit, or be
allowed to run with, the ball; (iii) no player is to be allowed to
stand in or about his adversaries' goal 'below the ball'; (iv) the
player may catch the ball full-pitch and make a drop-kick (as
in the Harrow game). In a *Tonbridgian* for 1861 we read an
account by an O.T. of the game as it *used to be* played, before
the game was transferred from the gravel to the grass; so that
Fonblanque's Homeric affrays were already obsolete.

But all was not well with the Tonbridge game and in the
years 1867-69 it fares badly at the hands of critics, in spite of
the new rules. No wonder it was unlucky, for they played
thirteen a side, and Rule Thirteen, as one might expect, incurs
particular animadversion. It ran 'Anyone running with the
ball may be collared, charged, hacked over, or tripped up'.
Would it make the game less enjoyable, asks a humane correspondent, if the words 'hacked over' were omitted? Hacking
over has, he thinks, 'a bad effect on certain temperaments'. Another correspondent remarks on the 'needless ferocity' of Tonbridge football. Visiting teams have been overheard describing
it as a 'dirty game', and hinting that they will not visit again.
On the other side, 'Old Boys and Present Boys agree in thinking that there is no game like it'—which was perhaps the
opinion of the visiting teams. The upshot was that, by 1869,
we were discussing whether to adopt the Harrow, the Rugby,
or the Association game, and within two years the decision had

been made in favour of 'Rugger'. The Rugby Union rules and the Football Association (Soccer) rules were rapidly superseding local customs all over the country at this time. They were, no doubt, like so much else, a by-product of the railways. Once teams began travelling about to play matches some kind of uniformity was essential. By 1873 football is compulsory, with fines for wilful abstention ranging from a shilling to half a crown.

A few more athletic items. In 1858 for the first time the cricket eleven was a recognized body with special 'colours'. Its captain was H. St. J. Reade, subsequently captain of the Oxford XI and headmaster of Oundle. Hockey seems to have dropped out, but Athletic Sports were established in 1857. One of the items was quoit-throwing which, after a long interval, has now been revived—if a quoit is the same thing as a discus. A boat club was established and died the next year, and a rifle corps suffered the same fate. Subscriptions were collected for a gymnasium but afterwards spent on fives' courts. The first O.T. dinner (not quite an athletic event, no doubt) was held in 1859, though the O.T. Association was not founded till many years later. An O.T. dinner is important as a sign that Old Boys were beginning to think of themselves as life-members, so to speak, of the community in which they had been educated. This retrospective gregariousness was a direct result of the Arnoldian spirit, and it is said that Arnold's Old Boys were the first to think of themselves and call themselves 'Old Rugbeians'. The founder of the O.T. Dinner appears to have been T. Nottidge, a member of a family which has been faithful to the school through many generations and has contributed at least half a dozen boys to the school in the last few years.

Thus new things make their appearance in a decade (1858-68) when the school was perhaps developing more rapidly than ever before or since. We even hear of chemistry. 'The want of instruction in chemistry has long been felt in our school, seeing that it is a most important and delightful study. . . . This want has now been supplied (1861), but we cannot but feel that, in

addition to the lecturer, a working laboratory is also a necessity
. . . for, by the use of such a proper place, all accidents that
frequently arise in the course of chemical experiments, and
much destruction of property, may be avoided.' This suggests
that the chemistry of those days was almost as 'tough' as the
football. Another quarter of a century was to pass before Alfred
Earl arrived and brought to Tonbridge real education in the
natural sciences.

New things were coming, and old things going. In Welldon's last year a correspondent writes, 'I wish to say a few
words about the present disgraceful state of the Giant's Stride.
Now, as the Giant's Stride is our only *attempt* at a gymnasium,
and as it is so greatly frequented by the fellows (when it is in
good repair) I think it ought. . . .' We hear no more of the
Giant's Stride and perhaps it was never repaired. Perhaps Tonbridgians were already beginning to look down on the Giant's
Stride as unworthy of the dignity of a public school.

The two most essential Arnoldian institutions were the
chapel and the principle of entrusting powers of government
to a specific group of senior boys. Under Arnold these boys
were simply the sixth form. Other headmasters introduced a
system of selection with the ultimate result that these positions
of honour and trust went more often to athletic than to intellectual eminence. Welldon instituted 'prepostors' at Tonbridge,
and if the following from the *Tonbridgian* editorial of 1868
gives a true account, the system took a little while to settle
down. 'It is a remarkable illustration of the unpopularity of
this system that it is, as a rule, equally distasteful to those who
enjoy, and those who are debarred from, these privileges. The
dignity of the tall hat and emancipation from the restraints of
call or detention are acceptable enough, but when the thought
of the responsibility he is about to undertake presents itself, he
involuntarily shrinks from it. The position of a prepostor may
be of great advantage to its occupier and his school-fellows, but
the opportunities it affords are frequently neglected, if not
abused. . . . The causes of the failure of the system are fourfold:
first, want of principle on the part of the prepostors themselves;

secondly, they are not sufficiently encouraged and countenanced by the masters; thirdly, they are not backed up by the sixth; and lastly, their efforts are not appreciated by the school generally.'

Very different is the attitude of the editors to the chapel, as shown in the editorial of 1863. 'Those who were at school when the school went to the parish church twice every Sunday, to sit on uncomfortable pews and listen to dull sermons, will be able to draw a very pleasing contrast between those times and the present. They will remember the bullying unprincipled set which formed a prominent feature of the fifth form. They will remember the rebellious fourth form, and the overgrown louts of the lower school. The chapel was opened. On its first anniversary the fifth form bullies, the fourth form rebels, and the lower school louts were not to be found. It is to the chapel services and sermons alone that this wonderful change is to be ascribed.' It sounds almost too good to be true, and perhaps it should be said that the object of the article is to rebuke those who fail to realize the value of the chapel. There is also an observation in another editorial of about this date that the prepostor system was the best cure for bullying, so perhaps the credit for whatever reformation of manners there may have been should be divided between the praes and the chapel in equal proportion.

On the subject of chapel we find a complaint that the choice of hymns is too narrow and the same hymns too often recur, the writer citing 'Not all the blood of beasts' as a special offender. We still occasionally hear complaints along the same lines, but we have at least dropped this particular hymn from our repertoire.

Meanwhile Her Majesty's Government was beginning to stretch out a long arm in the direction of the public schools. There had been a time when the State had not concerned itself with education in any way whatever. It was the private concern of those who wanted it, and those who wanted it would get what they wanted, if they could pay for it, on the well-known economic principle that supply will meet demand. In 1833 the

Government had begun to make annual grants to the societies providing what we should now call elementary schools. In 1839 it had begun to inspect the schools it subsidized. Among the inspectors, from about 1850 onwards, was Matthew Arnold, son of the old headmaster of Rugby, famous still as a poet and essayist but in his own day also important as a critic of our haphazard methods of education. An elementary system was being built up under the control of the State. Long before the end of the century that system would become universal, free of charge, and compulsory. But a controlled and organized elementary system would be to some extent wasted if chaos prevailed above.

In 1850 royal commissions were appointed to report on the state of Oxford and Cambridge, and the reports were extremely critical. Legislation, spread over the next twenty years, interfered in many respects with the activities of the ancient universities. It would, for example, not have been possible, in 1870, for Mr. Welldon of Tonbridge to secure an Oxford doctor's degree by simple purchase, as he did after appointment to his headmastership.

Having tackled both elementary schools and universities the State began to look with a critical eye on the stage of education that lay between. In 1858 royal commissions were appointed to inquire into and report upon the state of affairs in nine selected schools of ancient foundation—Eton, Winchester, Westminster, Charterhouse, St. Paul's, Merchant Taylors, Harrow, Rugby and Shrewsbury.[1] As a result of the report drastic alterations in the constitutions of these schools, and in particular of their governing bodies, were carried out by the Public Schools Acts of 1864 and 1868. In 1864 another royal commission was appointed to inquire into the affairs of *all* other endowed schools, with power to appoint assistants to inspect

---

[1] Four of the schools were in London, for Charterhouse had not at that date moved to Godalming. The five provincial schools were no doubt selected as leading examples, and it illustrates the stability of things English that much the same schools would be selected to-day (with the addition of Marlborough, which however was not an old foundation, having started in 1841).

and report to it on each school requiring investigation. Thus Tonbridge underwent its first public inspection.

The inspector's report pays generous tribute to the classical teaching and to the personal influence of the headmaster on the moral tone of the school, but is in other respects critical. He remarks that the Founder's intentions were (i) to provide free instruction[1] in grammar to boys residing in Tonbridge and the adjacent country, and (ii) to benefit the town by bringing boarders to the houses of the headmaster *and the inhabitants*. He continues: 'The school having become rich by accident, the Founder's intentions have been disregarded in most points. The instruction is comparatively expensive, and it is not considered desirable that townspeople not being masters in the school should receive boarders.' He also, very rightly, condemns the system under which the leaving exhibitions were, in accordance with the ill-advised terms of the scheme of 1825, practically reserved for 'foundationers', i.e. the sons of local parents. He remarks that these local parents were not, for the most part, bona fide citizens of Tonbridge but people who had come to live there solely to enjoy the privileges of the foundation.[2]

On the basis of their inspector's report the commissioners themselves reported to the Government in 1867. We will not burden the reader with any of their official verbiage, though two interesting points of fact may be noted. First, the endowment at that date yielded an income of only £2,000, though it was increasing and, in the early years of the next century would be multiplied, some said by ten and others by forty. Secondly, the bills of non-foundationer boarders ranged from £128 to £70, the average being £95. The range of variation is far greater than prevails to-day, but the average figure, allowing for the changed value of money, shows that Tonbridge

---

[1] The writer probably misunderstood the founder's intentions. See page 14.

[2] Day boys have, of course, long lost their monopoly of the leaving exhibitions, but it is still true that most of the Day boys are of the class described by the inspector. When I was housemaster of Welldon House not a single member of the house had been born in Tonbridge—on the one occasion between 1932 and 1937 when I made the inquiry.

education was more expensive then than it is now though very much less was given in return for the fees.

The upshot was three positive recommendations: first, that the preferential claim of foundationers to the leaving exhibitions should be abolished: secondly, that 'second or third grade schools' should be provided out of the endowment for the educational requirements of the townsfolk and to fulfil what were (rightly or wrongly) supposed to have been the Founder's intentions: and thirdly, that the Skinners' Company should cease to be the Governors, and a new governing body set up, half the members of which might, perhaps, be nominated by the Skinners' Company.

This brought the Skinners into action, and in 1870 they issued a new scheme of their own for submission to the Government. This provided, as one would expect, that the Skinners should continue to govern the school. They add—'The Governors propose to found a second grade school at Tonbridge or some adjacent locality, provided they are enabled to endow the same out of certain funds arising from the residuary estate of Sir Thomas Smythe and certain other funds possessed by the Company.'

Thus matters stood, and for some time continued to stand. In a *Tonbridgian* of 1871 the editors remark, 'We must look forward to great changes in our school administration in the next few years. The annual visitation of the Skinners' Company which is now taking place may very probably be the last, or nearly the last, anniversary of that event.' But events were not to move so fast, or so far, as these boys supposed. In 1873 Dr. Welldon and his staff addressed a circular letter to Members of the House of Commons, declaring that the school was suffering from the uncertainties and the controversies surrounding its future, and begging the recipients of the letter to exert their influence in favour of a speedy settlement. Nothing happened. In 1874 the Gladstone government fell. The Conservatives under Disraeli came into power and the whole business looked like being adjourned *sine die*.

In these circumstances Dr. Welldon, now in his sixty-fifth

year (1875) decided to retire. Whether he was a greater man than all his predecessors, who shall say? He had greater opportunities, and he made the best of them. He was not, like Arnold or Thring, a man of intellectual eminence, but he had in full measure that Evangelical fervour, that Roman *gravitas*, which was in those days, and is perhaps always, a more important element in successful headmastership than any merely intellectual gifts. When he died, twenty-one years later, many of his Old Boys contributed recollections to the *Tonbridgian*, from which the following fragmentary quotations may perhaps give a fair impression.

'It was Dr. Welldon's custom to take every form in the school once a month. The cane was always within reach on these occasions. . . . There is little doubt that the character of the school for discipline stood very high. . . . He was a strict master of the old school. I cannot say I remember him to have inspired me with new ideas. His mind was not speculative nor intellectually stimulating, but he was a sound scholar and a maker of sound scholars. He had a great memory for quotations, especially from Horace and Shakespeare. . . . His sermons were pithy and pointed, diversified with a few favourite aphorisms. They held the attention of his audience, and were always addressed to "my lads" or "my friends." . . . His habits of exercise and hydropathic treatment (he was a worshipper of cold water in every form) allowed him little time for reading, and he is said to have owned himself content if he were left with no more books than three—the Bible, Shakespeare, and Blunt's *Undesigned Coincidences*. . . . He was rigid in his ways, and when I knew him in 1860 he would not tolerate tobacco or an eyeglass. . . . He used to go for a walk before seven o'clock a.m. chapel, in which I occasionally joined him. Once, when we saw a brewer's dray going out, he remarked, "The devil always gets up early in the morning, sir". . . . When I applied to join the staff I showed him my testimonial from the headmaster I was then serving. "You had better put that in the fire, sir", was the remark that reached my astonished ears. . . . He was a very just man and a very charitably minded man, who

put the best construction upon men. He spoke ill of no one. . . .
He tolerated his assistant masters long and kindly.'

The part about the brewer is the more remarkable as Welldon, on his mother's side, belonged to the well-known brewing
family of Ind. But it would be easy to cite other Victorian examples of members of brewing families becoming bigoted tee-
totallers and thus, as it were, biting the hand that had fed them.

Rivington's *History* prints a long account of school days
under Welldon from the pen of the Rev. T. F. Burra who was
in the school from 1857 to 1862, of which this is the final paragraph. 'The Doctor stands out as a schoolmaster of the Arnold
type, encouraging a manly, straightforward tone, and as a warm-
hearted personal friend. No one this side of the grave will ever
know of the countless acts of generosity the old schoolmaster
exhibited; and his brother Edward was equally good. I can
remember my confirmation. The archbishop (Sumner) came
(with a wig) and though I remember nothing of his charge
except the wig I recall how I went up on to the "Head" near
"*Hanc aream aequandam curavit*" and vowed I was to be a good
man, and looked back on the old Parish Church in the dis-
tance. And now, at fifty or more, when I again look back, I can
fairly say that if I did not turn out all I intended it was certainly
not the fault of Tonbridge School, or of the good and great old
chief who then presided over its destinies.'

One more paragraph, in a lighter vein, and we must leave
this, the most epoch-making of all Tonbridge headmasterships.

'The doctor's hand-writing was completely illegible. At
the time of the starting of the *Tonbridgian*, hearing that Clap-
ham Grammar School produced a school magazine, he wrote
to the editor for advice. The letter was duly received and suit-
ably acknowledged, but the Doctor was none the wiser. The
editor would have been only too glad to assist, could he have
read the doctor's letter. Old Tonbridgians used to say that the
doctor wrote with a barge-pole. Four words only were de-
ciphered, and they were "School House, Tonbridge, Kent".
They happened to be in print. The editor, in addressing his

reply, pasted the illegible signature of the letter he had received on to an envelope and added the address below it. . . . Dr. Welldon did *not* write with a barge-pole, but with a quill pen, and many even now will recollect, when the pen refused to act, the drawing of it forcibly along the table, and the satisfactory grunt at the success of this remedy. The nib was invariably split, the blots and double strokes made confusion worse confounded, and it was absolutely impossible to make out the Johnsonian notices he sent round in the Detention Book.'

This from a letter signed 'P' in the *Tonbridgian* for August 1902.

Dr. Welldon's brother and Second Master, the Rev. Edward Ind Welldon, died in harness at Judde House (Old Judde) four years later. The two men regarded themselves as partners in the service of the school. No more 'Second Masters' have been appointed, though the senior assistant master acts as the headmaster's representative during periods of absence or illness.

V. MID-VICTORIAN ECHOES

We have already made considerable use of the *Tonbridgian*, but we have by no means exhausted the rich store of information that it contains about the school under Dr. Welldon and we propose in the present chapter to offer the reader a good deal more, much of it apparently trivial but all of it we think significant. *Litera scripta manet.* In these artless pages the mid-Victorian school seems to come to life again. Yet there are over two thousand of them—pages, we mean—and few will have the hardihood to read (or skip) through them from start to finish. We have performed this feat, and we offer the reader some of the fruits of our labours.

First as to the style of the paper itself. It was issued, in twelve-page numbers without a cover, *ten times* a year, an issue for every month except January and September. The editors, usually five boys, often groan audibly under the weight of their labours, but for the most part they doubtless enjoyed them. There was then very little teaching of 'English' in the school, and masters did not demand 'essays' from their forms with the dreadful regularity now prevailing. The columns of the *Tonbridgian* provided an outlet for those, never a negligible number, who wanted to write, not Latin and Greek, but their own language. The average issue opens with not one, but more often two or three, editorial 'leading articles'. These not only ventilate grievances and discuss, with a freedom which would probably not be tolerated to-day, the shortcomings of 'the authorities'. They also discuss, in a style apparently modelled on that of *The Times*, the public affairs of the day.

Next follow reports of cricket or football matches, and after these come what the French would appropriately call *pièces de résistance*—long essays on any conceivable learned subject, from the tin mines of Cornwall to the date of the siege of Troy. The record, we think, is held by a nine-column essay on the eighteenth-century philosopher, David Hume. There is also an article on the Talmud so weighty that it is treated as a serial and spread over two—or was it three?—issues. Who wrote these essays? The editors themselves, as a rule, and sometimes ex-editors in residence at Oxford or Cambridge. There is no evidence that any were written by masters, though of course some may have been. Indeed there is no evidence of magisterial interference with the paper at all, least of all by way of censorship. Opinions are often expressed which must have caused annoyance or even given pain to Dr. Welldon, but the nineteenth century was much more firmly convinced of the value of liberty than is its successor. Who read these essays? their authors, with avidity no doubt. Why were they inserted? to fill up space. That is always the editorial nightmare: to get the twenty-four columns filled somehow, and issued by the opening of next month.

Then there is verse. Occasionally the light verse is surprisingly good, and we hope it was original. On one occasion a contributor is rebuked for sending in a piece he had 'cribbed' from *Sabrinae Corolla*, which was the anthology of English verse used for Latin and Greek verse composition. When at a loss for a subject, the poets translate an Ode of Horace or a passage of Homer into English verse, or even translate a hymn into Horatian Sapphics. One gets a pleasing impression of a little community culturally unified by its concentration on a single course of study, the intensive study of a small selection of classical masterpieces. Thus, for example, when the editors remark, in connexion with the publication of the first edition of Septimus Rivington's *History of the School*, that Tonbridge will no longer be like the brave men before Agamemnon, we like to presume that everyone who mattered understood the allusion and found himself sub-consciously murmuring *Vixere fortes*; but if to-day an editor ventured on such a flight, how many boys—or masters—would know what he was after? Those were the days when Gladstone could quote seven consecutive lines of Lucretius in the House of Commons without being interrupted with cries of 'translate'. *Nous avons changé tout cela* (we still know French)—for the better, of course.

And lastly, correspondence. Every issue contains letters, half a dozen perhaps on an average, nearly all of them ventilating grievances, and as the same grievances are ventilated again and again, we gather that hope sprang eternal in the mid-Victorian breast. Perhaps the two most persistent grievances all through these seventeen years were—why have we no gymnasium? and, why aren't the day boys compelled to subscribe, like the boarders, to the *Tonbridgian?* The answer to the first question was—no money. The answer to the second was—we have no idea what the answer can have been. Apparently much less than half the day boys subscribed. One wonders whether they borrowed from the boarders or just did without it.

So much for the paper itself. It is difficult to know where to begin with the far too voluminous quotations we have collected, but perhaps the account of Skinners' Day 1858 will serve as a starting-point.

'The enjoyments of the last two days of the summer term were commenced by a large and hilarious breakfast party, consisting of the members of the Debating Society. . . . The party broke up in time to welcome the Skinners' deputation. . . . The number of scholars was found, on calling over, to be 163.'

This formal calling over of the school, by the headmaster in the presence of the Governors, continued until about 1935, when it was abolished in favour of the present morning address by the Master. No doubt its original purpose was to prove to the Governors that the boys asserted by the headmaster to be members of the school did in fact exist.

There is a good deal of free criticism of Skinners' Day proceedings in the years that follow. For example, in 1862, 'there was one circumstance which gave general umbrage to the school—the substitution of the gold and silver pens as prizes for the three first monitors in the place of books. As everything in the shape of argument and remonstrance has failed to rectify this great error on the part of the Skinners' Company we feel that it is useless to push our complaints further; but we shall never cease to regret that those magnificent prizes which, till quite lately, were awarded have been supplanted by the incompetent and comparatively worthless articles. . . .' Sir Andrew Judde in his statutes ordained the presentation of pens, but it looks as if the custom had died out long before and was now revived by some unpopular and (it is alleged) parsimonious antiquarian.

Another complaint is of the dullness of the proceedings, and that not without reason, for it was the statutory duty of the unfortunate examiner to conduct, in the presence of the Governors, a viva voce examination of every single boy in the school. Tonbridgians have heard that other schools have a 'Speech Day', and, not having one themselves, they imagine that it must be something very delectable. Demand arises for a 'Speech Day', either separate from or incorporated within the Skinners' Day programme. The demand is actually granted, and a performance staged exactly similar to that which prevailed at Harrow when the present writer was a member of that school, to wit, the enactment of scenes from Greek, French and English plays, Aristophanes, Molière and Sheridan being the authors preferred. If proceedings were on the Harrow model, the actors would perform in their ordinary school dress, with merely symbolical additions to indicate female characters. It need not be assumed that, on this account, the acting was poor. Good acting can be as independent of realistic costume as of realistic scenery.

There was a rather curious incident on Skinners' Day 1874. It was apparently the custom in those days that, at some stage in the prize-giving, the head boy made a presentation on behalf of the school to any assistant master who might be retiring from active service. On this occasion such a presentation was made to Mr. —— 'who has ever shown himself ready to assist in all matters in which the schoolboys themselves take interest. . . . Mr. —— replied in a speech full of feeling, and containing some good advice which was received with enthusiastic cheering. . . . The Head Skinner had previously given notice that this was the last occasion on which a testimonial could be allowed to be presented during the distribution of prizes.' The editor then proceeds to quote some strong language from a local paper censuring the Skinners, and suggesting that they must 'feel half ashamed' of their action.

I once asked my old friend Mr. Goggs, who was of course already a member of the staff, about this incident and he told me that there was more in it than met the eye of a modern reader of the old *Tonbridgians*; that Mr. —— had been more popular with the boys than with the masters and that his departure was not a matter of his own initiative; that the proceedings and the cheers were in fact a vote of censure on 'the authorities'. It is none the less very odd that these same authorities should not have disallowed this particular presentation instead of disallowing all subsequent ones; and the article from which we have quoted remains a remarkable example of Victorian 'freedom of the press'.

We have lingered too long on Skinners' Day. Let us pass to the Debating Society, which we have already encountered breakfasting. The society also debated with great assiduity, though of course it periodically died, and was revived after much tribulation in the correspondence columns. It is amusing to watch the procession of mid-Victorian figures at home and abroad, Gladstone and Disraeli, Garibaldi and Napoleon III, Lincoln and Bismarck, as they pass under the review of the sententious schoolboy. There is also a debate applauding and regretting the recent abolition of the Guy Fawkes' Day bonfire. Disinterested members regret it largely because it gave so much pleasure to our neighbours in the town, but offer them in exchange the consoling thought that they will soon be able to attend services in the about-to-be-erected School Chapel.

When at a loss for a novel subject the debaters sharpen their teeth on one or other of those classic bones of contention—was Cromwell justified in executing Charles I or Elizabeth in executing Mary Queen of Scots? The zest with which they attack such historical themes is remarkable; no doubt their natural appetite for history was not blunted by regular meals served up by the masters.

Then there is that most interesting assertion, debated again and again under one formula or another, 'that spirits do occasionally assume a visible shape and appear to men, which apparitions are commonly called ghosts'. On what lines would modern youth propose a motion such as this? Certainly not along the lines pursued by the boy Isaacson in 1858 who 'began by proving the existence of spiritual in distinction to corporal bodies from 1 Cor. xv, 44; the antiquity of the belief in the appearance of spirits from Matt. xiv, 26 and Acts xii, 15; that Christ countenanced the belief, from Luke xxiv, 39; and adduced instances of such appearances from 1 Sam. xxviii', etc. No doubt their Bibles meant much more to these boys than they do to most of us, and the debates occasionally remind us of that narrow Victorian Puritanism against which the leaders of Victorian thought were themselves in revolt. Motions condemning novel-reading and theatre-going as 'deleterious habits' are discussed and even carried.

Occasionally the modern reader is really surprised, as for example by the motion (carried by three votes) that 'Mr. Seymour Haydon's method of cremation is preferable to burial'. We are told that a clergyman had recently written an entertaining novel on the subject.

The building of the chapel involved the establishment of a choir which in its early years received a great deal of attention, the peformance of the tenors in, say, the Dykes in F Magnificat being discussed almost as gravely as the performance of the school batsmen in the match against Brighton College. The choir was encouraged by an annual supper followed by songs and other festivities, though in 1865, as the supper got postponed until after the beginning of Lent, the festivities were, of course, confined to 'sacred music'. This traditional respect for Lent has only been abandoned in comparatively recent years. As late as the 1920's the so-called O.T.C. sing-song had to be held before Lent began; after Ash Wednesday it would have been accounted improper. To-day our observance of Lent is no longer compulsory and negative but voluntary and positive.

There was also the Annual Concert, founded in 1853, five years before the *Tonbridgian* itself. Every year as the end of the Christmas term approached, the school, if we may believe the *Tonbridgian* editorials, worked itself up into a frenzy of excitement over this forthcoming event. Every December issue expresses hopes and fears and every February issue records that the concert was 'probably the best ever given'. The programmes are printed in full, and are to the modern eye a dreadful revelation, nothing but an endless succession of ballads, comic or sentimental, by deservedly forgotten composers, interspersed with a few trivial pianoforte solos and duets. The renaissance of music in England had not yet begun. Still, 'Messiah' and 'Elijah' were popular classics up and down the country, but we hear nothing of the singing of their choruses at Tonbridge.

What of an orchestra? In December 1860 we read that Dr. Welldon, 'who is ever anxious for the improvement of the school, not only in learning, but in gentlemanly character and all the *bienséances* of life, proposed what all would most gladly see fairly set on foot, viz. the establishment of a brass band'. This puts the moral values of the sackbut as high as anyone would wish, but, alas, nothing seems to have come of it. That brass band was like the piping of the flute-player on Keats's 'Grecian Urn'. No one ever squirmed under its performances. Again and again is the reader of old *Tonbridgians* thus tantalized. Something or other is advocated—a boat club, it may be, or a rifle corps—and its merits so carefully canvassed that the reader begins to believe it must be really just round the corner. Then one discovers a few years later that it had never been established at all, and the advocacy and discussion all begin again. Tonbridge School was progressing, no doubt, but not nearly as fast as ardent youth desired.

F

As regards games, I see that, when the *Tonbridgian* started, the practice, familiar to readers of *Tom Brown*, of herding all the small boys in goal while their betters indulged in active football, was still in use. It is attacked on good grounds and defended on bad ones. In 1864, however, 'all goal fagging, except for a few matches such as School House, etc. is abolished, and the goal will play on a ground of their own. May the fags show themselves worthy of their emancipation'. Rugger, as recorded in the previous chapter, was adopted in place of the disorderly and barbarous old Tonbridge game, in 1870, but the School continued to produce a XIII and not a XV for match purposes. Four 'hand-fives' courts were built, the only court game previously available being 'bat-fives', which must have been a primitive variety of squash. We read of the paper-chase and the steeple-chase, presumably different names for the same event. It was an arduous affair. On one occasion the hounds set a course of twelve and a half miles and on another they were out for three and a half hours. The writer who describes the second of these runs recommends a shorter course and a higher speed. No doubt at some later date, which research could determine but I have not, these vagaries were eliminated by the abolition of the hare and hounds' technique and the scheduling of the course in advance. Thus the paper-chase or steeple-chase became 'the Cras', a competitive cross-country race over a six-mile course. The curious name 'Cras' is said to be no older than about 1910 and to have derived from the curious pronunciation of some school character of that date.

.The rest of my material is so miscellaneous that I propose to present it to the reader as it presented itself to me, year by year.

1859. 'The merry festival of St. Valentine is now rapidly approaching; a day important to all, but more than all to schoolboys. On the eve of this occasion a great stir takes place among the small fry, for almost every individual among them makes a point of expending a share of his means and liberality on a valentine, and this for no other than the object of his "love at first sight". . . . Another order of boys, who have arrived at a more advanced point of their existence, may be found investing in gorgeously spangled and embroidered emblems of the day, which are to be carefully inscribed and posted to affectionate cousins,' and much more to the same effect, after which the origin of the festival is traced back, I dare say correctly, to the Roman Lupercalia, mentioned in Shakespeare's *Julius Caesar*. Another item of this year is a little poem congratulating Queen Victoria on the birth of her first grandson, afterwards the Kaiser who made war on us in 1914.

1860. Everyone knows that in those days the masters had 'mutton-chop' whiskers, but it is not perhaps realized that the boys sought to follow their example. A rather too facetious article proves what is in any case proved by house-groups and eleven-groups of the period. The fortunately hirsute youth is said to 'pull his whiskers with an air of ineffable superiority'.

1861. Under the title 'Tonbridge Traditions' a contributor deplores the fact that the tradition that Mr. Cawthorn's ghost haunts School House on the anniversary of his death has fallen into oblivion. 'Our predecessors felt very differently on this subject; and the terror of the youngest boys on the fateful night was such that the dormitory maid many years ago used to sit up with them until they went to sleep. This she assured me herself.' This is a pretty picture, and it raises in my mind the somewhat irrelevant question—Did school houses have matrons in those days? Probably not of the calibre we enjoy to-day. The duties now assigned to the matron would be divided between the housemaster's wife or housekeeper and some trusted domestic servant.

1864. In this year the Debating Society decided by fourteen votes to eight in favour of declaring war on Germany in defence of the Danish claim to the Duchies of Schleswig-Holstein. This was the first of the aggressive wars of modern Germany, and if Lord Palmerston's government and the House of Commons had held the same views as our Debating Society, the German Upas tree might have been nipped in the bud—'or else it might not, I cannot be positive which', as the poet says.

1865. A Public Schools' Calendar, no doubt an ancestor of the present *Public Schools Year Book*, has been published, containing accounts of twenty-three schools but omitting Tonbridge, the reason being that our numbers are too small. We have grown, but we must grow faster. The erection of the new buildings had not brought the expected increase; indeed the rate of increase had slowed down to something like a standstill. Perhaps we want a new and really commodious boarding house. (Park House, the first house outside the school grounds, was opened two years later.) The editors think that the severest handicap on the school is the restriction of the valuable leaving exhibitions to Foundationers, which in effect meant day boys. This ill-advised provision of the scheme of 1826 is a source of a most continuous discussion and complaint till its abolition in 1880.

There are some interesting remarks about school dress. 'Ten years ago the style of dress prevalent here was primitive in the extreme. The only respectable portion of the congregation were the monitors who walked about in solemn tail coats and wore very tall hats. The rest of the school wore short round jackets, and nether garments with one or more circular patches. . . . At last the monitorial uniform was abolished', and its abolition seems to have been due to the action of a 'bold bad monitor' who came to school in a short coat and found that the authorities had no objection. 'Since that day we have been allowed to wear what we like with the single exception of very light coats.' There is also a letter protesting against the misuse of what we take to be trouser pockets, as receptacles for the hands:—

'We can all remember the introduction of French pockets into this country and the immense sensation they created at the time. The ingenuity of generations had been taxed to furnish a pocket at once useful and ornamental, but in vain. At last a great nation had come forward as one man and supplied the want. It sent forth its pocket and the world received it with acclamation.' But there is another side to the picture. 'There is no doubt that these pockets encourage lounging. A schoolboy never likes to see his hands idle. He don't like to have them look him in the face and say, why don't you get me something to do? And when he buries his little counsellors in his pockets he buries all thoughts of work with them. . . . And moreover it is an unmannerly habit. There are little decencies of society which ought to be observed by boys as much as by men.'

During this and the preceding year the *Tonbridgian* was enlivened by the contributions of a brilliantly clever boy who used the pseudonym 'Van Drusen'. I wonder who he was and what became of him. I made inquiry on this subject in a *Tonbridgian* of 1923, and got no reply, and it is much more unlikely that I shall discover his identity now.

1870. Criticism concentrates for the moment on the school bathing place. 'We cannot doubt that the place called the Locks is very fit for bathing. The basin is close at hand for those who cannot swim at all, whilst there are many places above the Locks where those who cannot swim well can be in their depth, and those who can swim well get now and then the enjoyment of a "filling basin". There are also the Lock gates and the Lock arm for those who aspire to taking headers. Still, there are many things to be said against the Locks. Firstly, when barges go down the river, they always bring down the tar with them, and it is not pleasant to find oneself covered with tar. Secondly, the water is not nearly so clear as it is above the town . . . and we should be much rejoiced by hearing some day that a place above the town had been secured for the school bathing place.' This last point is expressed more bluntly by a poet who, impersonating the Medway, makes the river say, along with much else:

> *Truly, I receive some sewage,*
> *Truly, I'm the drain of Tonbridge.*

We also begin to hear at about this time that the chapel is overcrowded by visitors and that boys are often turned out of their seats and sent to overcrowd other seats, in order to make room for them. The school is also beginning to be irked by the custom of attending the parish church on Sunday mornings.

As we have had our own chapel for more than ten years why cannot we have all our services in it? Soon after this, Confirmation and Holy Communion began to be celebrated in the school chapel for the first time.

1871. We still have no rifle corps, no boat club, no gymnasium, and no natural history society, amenities enjoyed by so many schools with which we should like to claim equality. Shortly after this a 'drill corps' was started, without uniforms or rifles. As for a boat club, the school was held to be neither large enough nor rich enough to support an efficient boat club without injury to the cricket. Those who wished were allowed to join the town boat club, which is commended as a satisfactory institution.

'The usual monotony of school routine during a long summer term has this year been agreeably broken by the mid-term mathematical examination.' How easy it was to please our ancestors! This event, however, is evidence of the activity of the new mathematical master, Mr. Hilary (1870-1908), one of the ablest men who ever served the school, as an assistant master—or as a headmaster, for that matter. Henceforth mathematics competed strenuously with classics for the attention of the abler boys—too strenuously, some classically-minded contributors think. We also hear that French is being taken more seriously, though the attempt to establish chemistry as a school subject had long ago faded out. Parents, however, are said to be 'beginning to be clamorous' about the absence of a Science department, and a public-spirited person offers £50 to open a subscription list for the building of a laboratory.

1872. If we cannot get new school subjects we can at any rate get new school desks. Unfortunately these new desks have a very strong smell. Nor is that their only drawback. 'If a sheet of paper is laid on the desk for a few minutes a delicate transparency is imparted to it. . . . May we hope that a like transparency is not imparted to those parts of our clothing which come in close contact with the seats of these same desks.'

1874. A Gladstonian editor deplores in no measured terms the defeat of his idol in the general election of this year, and that not on national grounds only. The victory of the Tories, he opines, gives the death-blow for the time being to the school's chances of getting a revised scheme from the Endowed Schools' Commission, which will set it free from the cramping tyranny of the 1825 constitution. Uppingham and Repton, to mention only two, have obtained new constitutions but we have not, and we shall have to wait till the Liberals come in again. Thus the editors, in a long and able article, which finds confirmation in the pages of the first authoritative history of English education I have consulted, namely *The Silent Social Revolution* by G. A. Lowndes (1937). In a subsequent editorial we are told, whether rightly I know not, that the new Tonbridge scheme had been prepared some time before but had been held up owing to disagreement between the Commissioners and the Skinners' Company as to the composition of the new body of governors.

However, if progress is checked in one direction, it finds outlets in another. In the very next year the now famous Joint Board began to hold examinations for the awarding of school certificates. It was a long time, however, before 'school cert.' assumed either its present form or its present importance. Indeed, the Certificate examination established in 1874 was what we should now call 'Higher Cert.', a gentlemanly affair designed for Sixth forms.

1875. The teaching of phonography, the new and improved method of shorthand, is recommended by a correspondent.

Meanwhile the time has come for Dr. Welldon to retire, and the many achievements of his long reign can be viewed in appreciative retrospect. There is no doubt that, in spite of the postponement of our new scheme of government, in spite of the absence of a gymnasium in our grounds and the presence of sewage in our bathing place, it's a grand old school and we are proud to belong to it. This last year has brought us more university honours than any of its predecessors. But that does not alter the fact that the school drinking-fountain is out of order. What is the use, says a correspondent, of an inscription telling you in Greek that 'water is best', if in fact you can't get any?

VI. MR. ROWE AND DR. WOOD—AND A
DIGRESSION (1876-98)

I n succession to Dr. Welldon the Governors appointed
the Rev. Theophilus Rowe (1876-90), who had been for
some years a housemaster at Uppingham, then at the
height of its fame under Thring. The principle they evidently followed is in many respects a sound one. The selection
committee of a governing body find themselves confronted
with a number of candidates, several of whom seem equally
favourable specimens of the sub-species *homo sapiens paedago-
gicus*. They hardly know which will prove best in practice, and
testimonials are too laudatory to be very helpful. So they say
to themselves, 'Mr. X. comes from ——— which, under the
famous Y., has the reputation of being the best public school
in England. If we appoint X. he will surely bring to our school
all the good things that have made the present reputation of
———.' That is all very well; but if X. has little to recommend
him *except* his years of service at ———, the results will not be
equivalent to expectations. It would be easy but indiscreet to
quote, from the experience of other schools than Tonbridge,
appointments made on these lines which have turned out
badly.

Mr. Rowe was in many respects an enlightened man, more
up to date in his ideas than Dr. Welldon perhaps. But he was
not nearly so successful a headmaster. 'Though a fine scholar',
we are told, 'an inspiring teacher and an amiable character, he
was afflicted with an intellectual honesty which impelled him

86

to say exactly what he thought about people and things at all times, convenient and inconvenient, and he sometimes gave utterance to his real thoughts on occasions when more worldly guile would have dictated reticence.' Such qualities sometimes go with a strong, dominating character and prove effective even when they are disconcerting. Not the least successful of Victorian prime ministers was famous for his 'blazing indiscretions'. But Mr. Rowe had not a dominating character. He was not much of a disciplinarian. 'That man does make me sweat' was the remark of an Eton boy after an interview with the great Dr. Warre. Mr. Rowe was not at all like Dr. Warre.

However, circumstances over which Mr. Rowe had no control made the period of his headmastership an exceptionally difficult one.

Under Disraeli's government the Charity Commissioners had taken over the unfinished undertakings of the now defunct Endowed Schools Commission. As regards the Tonbridge problem there was a tangle of issues at stake. Were the Skinners to retain their position as governors? where was the money for the new 'second grade' school to come from—the Tonbridge School endowment, other funds controlled by the Skinners, or the public purse? and where was the new school to be, Tonbridge or Tunbridge Wells? The latter was the larger town and, being within the ancient parish of Tonbridge, it might be maintained that it was within the orbit of the Founder's beneficent intentions. It should perhaps be said that, at the time we are concerned with, the modern type of County Secondary School, controlled and maintained by public education authorities, did not exist. Such schools were only made possible by the Education Act of 1902. In the nineteenth century, though elementary education was already becoming mainly a State concern, there was no secondary education except that provided by private schools (of a type now almost extinct) and 'public' schools, which were, and are, 'public' only in the sense that they were not the personal property of individuals.

Roughly speaking, it would be true to say that, in 1876, the

Commissioners, realizing that the Skinners' Company were extremely anxious to retain control of their old school, put pressure upon them to find adequate endowment from their other funds for the new school, and then decreed that this new school was to be at Tunbridge Wells. It was founded in 1887 and is known as the Skinners' School. Its headmaster for many years was the Rev. F. G. Knott, father of two of the finest cricketers produced by Tonbridge School, one of whom has been a master at his old school since 1925.

This left Tonbridge town in the lurch. It appealed to the Commissioners and the latter applied to the Skinners' Company, who undertook to finance another 'second grade' school in Tonbridge, this time at the expense of the Andrew Judde endowment. This could only be done by somewhat drastically curtailing for several years expenditure on the old school. The Judd School, as it is called, was founded in 1888.

Meanwhile the new scheme for our own school had come into operation in 1880, superseding that of 1825 as that of 1825 had superseded the Statutes of the Founder. The Skinners' Company emerged, battered but triumphant, retaining unimpaired their ancient trusteeship. It is said, with what truth I know not, that Tonbridge alone of the old public schools retains exactly the governing body of its sixteenth-century foundation.

The editors of the *Tonbridgian*, who had often, as we have observed, criticized the Skinners' Company somewhat trenchantly, express their satisfaction. 'The school has every reason to rejoice that it will continue to be governed by the Company, instead of passing under a heterogeneous body of gentlemen, possessing no separate corporate character, and having no tradition to connect them either with the school or with each other. . . . Ought not the school to be allowed an extra half-holiday or two to commemorate it?'

For those who appreciate the historical continuity which is so characteristic a feature of English institutions the decision to preserve our ancient constitution intact was and is gratifying. None the less the thoughtful reader may incline to ask himself, or even to ask the present writer, whether it was what the authors of 1066 *and All That* call 'a good thing'.

There is always an insuperable difficulty in the way of giving a plain answer to such hypothetical questions. Was it, for example 'a good thing' that Disraeli instead of Gladstone won the General Election of 1874? Was it 'a good thing' that in 1792 the Austrian and Prussian armies failed to take advantage of their obvious opportunities and nip the new-born revolutionary French Republic in the bud? In neither case is a definite answer possible, for the question involves the comparison of a known with an unknown quantity. We know what happened; we do not know what might have happened. And in addition to this general difficulty the author labours under a special difficulty in answering the particular question which he imagines to be addressed to him in that he is a salaried servant of the employers whose merits the question invites him to discuss. None the less it seems permissible to offer a few tactful and innocuous remarks on the subject.

It might be maintained that all governing bodies of public schools, reformed and unreformed, suffer from being rather too remote from the institutions they have to govern. This point of view was put before me by one who is a governor of another public school and also, as a Fellow of an Oxford college, a governor of that same college. He held that his college was better governed than his school because the governors of the former were nearer to 'the object' than the governors of the latter, being for the most part the people who actually discharged its daily duties. This raises the rather thrilling question whether a public school could, in fact, be adequately governed by its staff, or a body selected by some method from its staff. But no: the idea must be dismissed as preposterous. The inferiority of schoolmasters to dons is too painfully apparent. We are left, then, with a choice between a remote governing body of the usual 'reformed' pattern and a governing body such as the Skinners' Company constitutes.

The governors of Tonbridge school are the Court of the Skinners' Company. The Court consists of about thirty members, recruited by the election of one member each year, from among the two hundred Liverymen of the Company, to the office of Renter Warden. Each Renter Warden proceeds through a series of four offices, each held for one year, to the supreme office of Master of the Company, after which year of glory he relapses into the comparative obscurity of a Past-Master, remaining a member of the Court for the rest of his life. The reason why the Court contains about thirty members must obviously be that Liverymen are elected to the Renter Wardenship when what insurance companies call their expectation of life is about thirty years. The Master will, therefore, be a man in the prime of life and not a dodderer who has come to the top by reason of the dubious virtue of longevity.

One of the obvious differences between the Court of the Skinners' Company and an ordinary governing body is that the latter has a permanent chairman, selected presumably for his business acumen and educational statesmanship, who holds office as long as he feels equal to the task. Sometimes such chairmen are of great value. I remember being shown round the present premises of Christ's Hospital by a former headmaster and being told by him that the buildings were as free from faults as school buildings could be, a boon which he attributed to the fact that the chairman of the Christ's Hospital governors at the time of the move had been Dr. Haig Brown, formerly headmaster of Charterhouse at the time when that school also made its move from London to the country. Haig Brown knew everything that had been done right and everything that had been done wrong on that former occasion. But this may well be an exceptionally favourable example. There have been, to my knowledge, chairmen of 'reformed' governing bodies for whose retirement headmasters and staffs have prayed long, earnestly and without result. I could cite the case of an enterprising young headmaster who, without neglecting the resource of prayer, set himself to drive his chairman into retirement by continuous botheration. He pestered the poor man with a long succession of knotty problems, by correspondence and personal visitation, and his prayers, thus reinforced, received the answer they deserved.

The chairman of the Tonbridge governors is the Master of the Skinners' Company and the Master holds office for one year only. If a Master should be inadequate to the task of school government—and I am far from asserting that there have ever been any such—then the school may console itself with the thought expressed by one of our poets in the words 'we suffer, but we shall not suffer long'. If, on the other hand, a Master is particularly well equipped for school government and is keen on the job it seems a pity that he should be removed from office just as he is getting into his stride. Such an one might well say to himself, 'Here am I, removed from office just as I was beginning to realize the things I wanted to get done'. It is true, of course, that such a man can continue to influence the government of the school as an ordinary member of the Company, but the opportunities of the Master, as chairman, must be unique and the loss of office must to a considerable extent mean the loss of power.

On the whole it may be surmised that a 'reformed' governing body *ought*, on paper calculations, to be a more efficient instrument than the Skinners' government as traditionally constituted but it may be doubted whether, on the average, it is so. For the Skinners enjoy certain impalpable advantages. They probably feel that their school belongs to them and is 'part of their show' more strongly than does the average governor of other schools. Many of them no doubt take little interest in the school except during their brief period of office as Master, and one need not claim that they are under any obligation to take such an interest; a man may have many legitimate reasons unconnected with school governance for seeking membership of the Court of a City Company. Others, by no means always old boys of the school, take a close and lifelong interest, attested by their annual presence on Skinners' Day. To such we should be, and are, grateful.

And what other governing body gives an annual dinner to its school staff, the local culinary efforts of the Rose and Crown being washed down—the verb seems unworthy of the occasion but I cannot think of another—by the priceless vintages of Dowgate Hill? *In vino veritas*. Observation suggests that the guests are more susceptible to these siren draughts than their hosts, not because they indulge more freely but because they lead lives of greater austerity on the other three hundred and sixty-four evenings of the year. We opened this rather ticklish discussion with the suggestion that all governing bodies were rather too remote from the object governed, but on the eve of Skinners' Day our governors come very near to us, and it may be that they learn more about us on those occasions than we can afterwards recall having told them.

And now let us resume the easy-going course of our history. First we must describe the changes made by the New Scheme, which came into operation in 1880. The old monopoly of the foundationers in the matter of the leaving exhibitions was abolished, and the age of entry raised from eight to ten. This last proved a curious miscalculation.[1] One of the conspicuous developments of the last quarter of the nineteenth century was the appearance, in large numbers, of the modern type of 'Preparatory School', competing with the public schools for the care of the pre-adolescent schoolboy. Some public schools, like Clifton and Oundle, retained their own 'prep. school department', as one may call it, under their own management. Others frankly let it go. Admission at ten was an impossible compromise, seeing that eight was the normal age for leaving the nursery governess or the co-educational infant school, in those days generally called a kindergarten. Numbers below the age of thirteen rapidly dwindled, and this was doubtless the main cause of the decline in the number of the school as a whole under Mr. Rowe. He started with 222 boys and ended with 181. Two new boarding-houses were started in his early years, Hill Side and Parkside, but it is obvious that the number of

---

[1] Right down to 1938 Tonbridge retained on its prospectus words indicating the age of admission as 'from 10 to 14'. On the rare occasions when parents tried to send boys of ten or eleven they had to be told that the prospectus was, in this particular, out of date.

boys in each of the five boarding-houses must have been small.

Boarding-houses in those days were started by their first housemasters at their own financial risk. They bought or built their houses and afterwards sold or rented them to their successors. The Governors did not buy them till well on in the present century. This seems very absurd, but it could be paralleled from the histories of many other public schools.

The new scheme emphasized the importance of widening the curriculum, at the same time abolishing the extra fees hitherto charged for several of the non-classical subjects. The chief need was science, and here Mr. Rowe got to work even before the scheme came into force. A science master was appointed, a laboratory for sixteen boys was fitted up and a Scientific Society was founded, which for some years published accounts of its transactions. Papers were read, by masters, boys or visitors, on subjects ranging from beetles to telepathy and from telepathy to sewage, this last being handled, if that is the right word, by the headmaster himself. The observatory, that now neglected item in the school equipment, was also built and for some years astronomy was a regular time-table subject. But all these activities were probably somewhat amateurish and sporadic until the apointment of Alfred Earl in 1884, who presided with brilliant success over the science side until his retirement in 1918.

No doubt Earl's success in kindling enthusiasm encouraged the Governors to find money for his subject, in spite of the financial stringency caused by the diversion of funds to the Judd School. On 24th May 1887, now known as Empire Day but then as the Queen's birthday, 'the opening of the splendid Science and Art Buildings took place', says the *Tonbridgian*. 'At one o'clock the School assembled to greet the Lord Mayor of London (an Old Tonbridgian) and the Court of Skinners. ... Eighty Old Boys were present. The company adjourned to the gymnasium where lunch was prepared. . . . At half-past two the procession started to the New Buildings, where the Lord Mayor unlocked the door and a tour of the rooms was made.' Speeches followed by the Master of the Skinners' Company, the Headmaster, the Lord Mayor and Sir Robert Ball, a famous astronomer of those days, who, rather unsuitably, delivered 'a sparkling and lengthy tirade' not only in favour of science but against classics. He described the learning of Latin and Greek as 'an absurd waste of time', which provoked a rejoinder from old Dr. Welldon who 'before hurrying off to catch his train hoped that classics might not fall into the background'. Then followed a concert at seven o'clock, opening with Dr. Stainer's new Jubilee Anthem; for Queen Victoria, as well as Tonbridge School, was holding celebrations that summer.

As a matter of fact Dr. Welldon's hopes were fulfilled and, for the next forty years, a balance was fairly maintained between the new and the old learning. There has scarcely ever been a year since that date, we believe, in which at least one boy, very often many more, has not gained a college entrance scholarship or exhibition in classics from the school. In recent years the classical side has become small and select and very few learn Greek who are wholly devoid of aptitude. Perhaps that is just as well. If classical studies die out in the future it will only be because boys, or their parents, fail to make use of the facilities generously offered for the best of all intellectual educations.

The building was known in those days as the Science and Art Building. The large room on the right, on the ground floor, became the library, and that above it became the Art School where, in 1890, Mr. Buckmaster began his record reign of fifty years on the staff of the school. This is a convenient place to mention that a *Tonbridgian* for 1878 records the death of Mr. Tattershall Dodd 'who for forty-four long years (1834-78) laboured within these walls imparting artistic skill'. He joined the staff when he was only nineteen, and some time in the 'fifties painted the delightful landscape of 'Cricket on the Head', which hangs in the headmaster's hall. There are several tinted engravings of the picture about the school, and more vividly perhaps than any written record it brings home, or ought to bring home, to present Tonbridgians something of the spirit of the old mid-Victorian schooldays. His son served the school as Lower Drawing-master during the first quarter of the present century. I used to urge him to stay till 1934 and complete the family century, but he did not feel equal to that.

Other new subjects also found their way into the life of the school. German was introduced. A gymnasium, so long looked forward to, was at last built, and four rooms, three of wood and one of corrugated iron, were set apart for workshops. Soon half the school were learning carpentry. We also hear of a photographic society, an ambulance class and a bicycle club. The bicycles must have been of the so-called 'penny-farthing' type. There can be no doubt that Mr. Rowe, in spite of his shortcomings as a disciplinarian, encouraged the stimulus of variety and new ideas.

In 1884 Tonbridge, like many other schools at about the same date, established a 'Mission', now more sensibly called a boy's club, in one of the slum areas of London, very properly choosing the parish of St. Pancras, from which the school draws most of its endowment. There is irony, some might say bitter irony, in the fact that the wealth of Sir Andrew Judde's school at Tonbridge should be so closely allied to the poverty of Judd Street and Tonbridge Street, W.C.1. The early 'eighties were a time of acute industrial distress, and in those days there was no unemployment insurance. The social conscience was awakened by many appeals, not least perhaps by those of General Booth, the founder of the Salvation Army. The rich responded with organized charity, the poor with movements which ultimately led to the foundation of the Labour Party.

Other new departures are adumbrated, a Tuck Shop and a School Rifle Corps. Tonbridge seems to have lagged behind many or most public schools in the matter of military training.

In 1877 the parish church was subjected to a long and drastic process of restoration, which apparently it badly needed. During a period of two years seating accommodation was limited and the school was excluded from the Sunday morning services which it had hitherto been obliged to attend. After 1878 attendance at the parish church was resumed but with much reluctance. The headmaster and his staff petitioned the Governors to secure their release from this ordinance of the Founder, who had of course never contemplated his school possessing a chapel of its own. The local clergy, very impertinently as it seemed to many at the school, responded with a counter petition. The Governors had secured, in the new scheme, the right to decide the matter for themselves, but release from this 'bondage', as Mr. Rivington calls it, was not granted until Dr. Wood's time. Before the restoration of the church the school had sat in a gallery on the north side, the Skinners' Gallery, where 'cooped up in a corner beneath the roof they endured every Sunday morning two hours of misery'.[1] The gallery was adorned by a wooden shield with the arms of the Skinners' Company, dated 1663. After the restoration of the church this shield was given to the headmaster and set over the doorway of the 'Skinners' Library', i.e. his dining-room.

The columns of the *Tonbridgian* throw some further light on the everyday life of the school under Mr. Rowe.

It is tempting to quote from the records of the debating society, but perhaps the temptation should be resisted. I will take the record of one year only, 1877-8. 'That the higher education of women is unnecessary'—lost 11-9; 'That museums and picture galleries should be opened to the public on Sundays'—lost 12-9; 'That trade unions are injurious to the country'—carried 15-4, only one boy, Harold Cox, afterwards a Liberal M.P. and two masters speaking against the motion.

We have reached a time in the history of the school when not only headmasters but assistant masters also take on flesh and blood and become distinguishable one from another. We cannot explore these personalities very far, but one testimonial seems worth quoting. In 1880 William McGill, O.T., left to take up a headmastership after being for sixteen years housemaster in School House. The editors write, 'We cannot but fear that his absence will involve the absence of many O.T.'s

---

[1] The histories of most public schools run on parallel lines. At Harrow in old days the boys were 'cooped up' in a similar gallery, and used to hang their watches over the front of it when they thought the sermon had gone on long enough.

who we believe come down to the school more to meet Mr.
McGill again than for anything else'. Sixty years have passed,
and to-day McGill is nothing more than a small tablet in the
ante-chapel which perhaps scarcely anyone now on the staff or
in the school has consciously noticed, but he must in his day
have been a splendid fellow and a great figure in the school.[1]
Truly 'our little life is rounded with a sleep'.

House matches begin to occur but, at cricket at any rate,
the housemasters are, or are allowed to be, members of their
sides. It is small wonder that the day boys A-K beat Hill Side,
seeing that Mr. Goggs made 77 for the day boys, 'a useful and
patient innings, not without faults', says the reporter, whereas
Mr. Ilbert for Hill Side made 3 and 0. Among extinct sports
must be classed 'double bat fives' and 'single bat fives'. There
were competitions in both these games in 1880. Also it is proposed that a bicycle race should be added to the Athletic Sports.

Some time during Rowe's headmastership, I have been told,
the *Tonbridgian* gave offence in some way or other and the
headmaster punished it by reducing it to its original status as a
magazine which no boy was compelled to purchase. It nearly
died of its punishment and perhaps that was what Rowe hoped
for. If so we may be thankful that his hopes were disappointed.
But how curious and interesting this is. If the *Tonbridgian* or any
other school magazine committed an impropriety to-day the
headmaster would tighten up the censorship as exercised by
himself or by an assistant master detailed for this duty, but he
would not dream of doing what Rowe did. The boys would
still be compelled to buy their school magazine and the magazine would be compelled to behave itself. But the Victorians
disliked compulsion. Rowe did not lay extra fetters on the
editors: he simply set free the purchasers.

On Mr. Rowe's resignation the Governors appointed Mr.
John Kennedy, Headmaster of Aldenham, who however
resigned before undertaking his duties, a proceeding adversely

---

[1] When McGill died in 1890 his friends made a handsome donation of books
to the School Library, all uniformly bound in brown morocco. It includes the
Dictionary of National Biography.

commented on in a 'not very polite paragraph' by the *Oxford Magazine*. Mr. Rowe consented in the circumstances to carry on for another term, and the Governors appointed Dr. Joseph Wood (1890-8), previously headmaster of Leamington.

Dr. Wood brought with him a number of Leamington boys, a fact which illustrates the confidence he must have inspired in the Leamington parents, though it may have been resented by the authorities of Leamington College. How Tonbridge felt about the invasion is not quite clear. The *Tonbridgian's* tactful comment is that 'the number of new faces— a large portion of them from the same school—is, we should imagine, unprecedented. And when we consider also how many new masters there are, it is evident that there is considerable novelty to which we must accustom ourselves'. The reader must decide for himself whether these words half conceal a shade of resentment. However that might be, the school prospered numerically as it had never done before. Dr. Wood started with 174 boys and in his eight years raised the numbers to 444, the maximum being then fixed at 450.

The new headmaster was a man of real distinction. Though we have no portraits of most of his predecessors we would hazard a guess that he was the handsomest of all Tonbridge headmasters.[1] His aquiline features were of the type that suggested a cardinal of the Roman Church, perhaps because they had points in common with those of the two great English cardinals of the Victorian Age, Newman and Manning. Wood's dignity, when he chose to assert it, would have sufficed for any earthly office from the papacy downwards. On horseback he was superb. The present writer was a boy under him at Harrow, whither he went as headmaster after leaving Tonbridge. Perhaps a few of my recollections may be excused, for though it was a different school it was the same man.

'Joey', as we called him, once took it into his head that he

---

[1] It is unfortunate that the portrait painted to commemorate his Tonbridge headmastership and now in the reading room (Old Big School) is a wretched daub. The photograph in Rivington's *History* gives a better idea of him, but is inadequate.

would like to read through the Iliad with a few boys. He picked about half a dozen from the classical upper sixth, let us off a fair amount of our ordinary form work, to the unconcealed annoyance of our form master, and got us to come round to his study at nine o'clock two or three evenings a week. There we sat in comfortable armchairs and translated in turn. 'Joey' also took his turn, and it was an education in more than one language to listen to him, for he was the most felicitous translator of Homer one can imagine. At ten o'clock he would say, 'Now, boys, let us have a little refreshment', and we would go to a table and get ourselves a slice of cake and a glass of claret. I have an idea the old man took a mischievous pleasure—for he was mischievous at times—in keeping us talking long enough to make us break the rigid rule which ordained that all boys in all circumstances had to be back in their houses by 10.30 p.m. I remember once being thus late and encountering my own housemaster in his hall—stark mad in pink pyjamas, to adapt a quotation from Sheridan.

As a preacher Wood could make a little go a long way. I remember an end of term sermon in which he repeated again and again the refrain 'For good or for evil, the term is *done*' until it achieved a positively shocking significance. I remember also his last sermon on the Sunday before he left. It began doubtless with the usual points about boys leaving school and going out into the world, the responsibilities of manhood, and so on. Then followed the unforgettable: 'A time comes for *all* of us to leave school; but I "must wear my rue with a difference".' Surely this deserves to rank high in any list of felicitous quotations.

I do not think Dr. Wood was a saint; I rather doubt if he was a deeply religious man; but he was an artist. Behind the façade of his dignity he looked out on life with a rather cynical humour. There is a Tonbridge story about one of his end of term reports. The housemaster had written, in the space provided for his remarks, 'I fear he does not always do his best'. In the headmaster's space next door there was added in his exquisitely neat lettering: 'Nor do I. J.W.' He rather delighted in oracular mystification, and it is said that Tonbridge boys used the term 'A Joey' to mean a remark which, while not exactly untrue, turned out to mean something different from what one had supposed.

The increase in numbers involved at first obvious inconvenience. 'There has been', said Dr. Wood, 'one master taking his form in the cricket pavilion, another in the gymnasium, while a third has even been relegated to a fives' court. I believe there was a hope that we should be obliged to send yet another form to the tuck shop.' These remarks occurred in a speech opening in 1894 the new school buildings, which connected up the old Welldon building of 1863 with the recent 'science and art' building of 1887 in one continuous whole, including the arch with its clock tower, the top room in which was used for music, and the New Big School. The *Tonbridgian* of that date shows a drawing of the whole by the architect, Mr. Campbell Jones, with Old Judde and the old chapel obliterated. The destruction of these buildings was part of the original plan, never carried out for obvious financial reasons. We do not regret their survival. Old Judde no doubt spoils the pattern, by reason both of its situation, its style, and its brick; but in itself it is a dignified and agreeable building, and an old school should preserve the visible memorials of its history. The incongruities of the total group of buildings are, after all, in the English tradition. Of all our old cathedrals only Salisbury, of all our old Oxford colleges only Wadham, is all of a piece. Truro cathedral and Keble college are also all of a piece, and who finds comfort in their contemplation?

Meanwhile both Old Judde and the old chapel were given new uses, the former as a sanatorium, the latter as a museum. The Judde House boys moved in 1893 to their present quarters under Mr. Whitby, and before the end of Dr. Wood's reign Ferox Hall was started under Mr. Earl and Manor House under Mr. Pott. Thus the tale of the boarding-houses was completed.

We have left till last what should chronologically have come first. The Governors and Dr. Wood wisely decided that a new chapel really worthy of the school was, like Rome, something that could not be built in a day, and a temporary chapel, 'this last product of the iron age' as the *Tonbridgian* calls it, was erected on land to the south of the headmaster's house. It served its purpose for ten years and was then demolished. The Solomon of the new Temple was to be not Dr. Wood but his successor, Dr. Tancock.

Additional space was also required for games. 'Martins' was purchased and also the field called 'the fifty' off the Shipbourne road. The rackets court was built and the swimming bath excavated. Hitherto bathing had been in the Medway, and complaints of the objects to be found in its waters had long been a stock subject for letters to the *Tonbridgian*, as we have seen.

The Volunteer Rifle Corps was also at long last established. It had been discussed off and on since 1860, when Napoleon III's annexation of Savoy and Nice suggested awful memories of the first Napoleon and inspired an agitation for 'volunteers' throughout the country. There was actually a short-lived Tonbridge volunteer corps in that year. T. F. Burra, who was then in the school, wrote long afterwards, 'The corps had a brief existence. We drilled in the playground and I can remember forming fours and marching about; but as we had no instruction in, or opportunity of, shooting the corps died a natural death'. Mr. Burra says nothing about the uniform. At some schools, the 1860 volunteer corps were dressed in the style of Garibaldi's famous Redshirts. There was also, as we have recorded, a rather dreary 'drill corps' without uniforms or rifles in the later days of Dr. Welldon, but this had also long been defunct.

To return to Dr. Wood's day—the new corps was of course voluntary, as were probably all school corps until the outbreak of the First Great War in 1914. The editors of the *Tonbridgian* venture to 'remind those patriotic youths who have already enrolled themselves that they have undertaken no sinecure; no, indeed, theirs is no easy task; the most strict and unremitting attention must be bestowed on their drill. . . . Persevere then, ye youthful band, and never let it be said that Tonbridge is lacking in patriotism.' It looks as if the editors had not joined.

Just as members of the choir are still rewarded for their labours by an extra half-holiday, so members of the corps were rewarded by an annual entertainment, got up for their amusement. When the corps became compulsory there was no need to reward the 'volunteers', but the entertainment has survived and is one of the most popular of Tonbridge institutions. Each house invents and stages its own 'show', for the entertainment of the rest. The officer in charge finds the organization of the 'Sing-song', as it is still misleadingly called, one of the most arduous but also one of the most amusing of his duties.

Dr. Wood began his headmastership with a most popular measure, the abolition of early school. 'On 29 July we shall go into chapel at 7 a.m. for the last time,' say the editors with such comment as can be well imagined. Henceforth there was to be preparation in the houses from seven to eight a.m. which survived (in the summer term only) till about 1921. Chapel was henceforth at 8.55, followed by four periods of morning school. Afternoon school was from 3.30 to 5.30 in winter, three times a week. At some later date which I have not determined the hours of afternoon school were altered and shortened, and the number of half-holidays reduced to two, but in 1940 the three-half-holiday week was re-established.

Another change was less popular at first, the substitution of caps marked with the house colours for the old 'collegers', or academical caps like those worn by masters. The editors of the *Tonbridgian* write 'Who designed the caps we do not know, but we are obliged to confess we think them extremely ugly. . . . The wearers resemble errand boys more than anything else.' But they have survived, for they are probably the most sensible headgear for schoolboys except one—namely, no headgear at all. At a later date straw hats were introduced for prepostors, and for general school use in summer. For a short time there were special black and white straw hats for Sunday use only.

About the same time a letter appeared in the *Tonbridgian* censuring the prepostors for going about with walking sticks!

'Several Old Boys have expressed their dissatisfaction and it is hoped the idea will die a natural death'. It did so; as did a still more exotic fashion taken up by certain prepostors ten years earlier, namely, the wearing of rings. Perhaps this was a Tonbridge offshoot of the aesthetic movement which devastated the *jeunesse dorée* in the early 'eighties and was satirized by Gilbert and Sullivan in *Patience*.

The abolition of early school was designed largely, perhaps wholly, for the convenience of the day boys. Certainly it led to a large increase in their numbers. In Mr. Rowe's last year they numbered 58 (out of 181), in Dr. Wood's last year 137 (out of 444). This was felt to be too many and the day boy maximum was subsequently fixed at 100. They were divided into two houses, at one time divided alphabetically, A to K and L to Z; afterwards on roughly geographical lines, day boys A being those who lived sufficiently near the school to go home for their meals, and day boys B being those for whom lunch and changing rooms were provided at the school. But this line of division was not rigidly observed. In 1932, to complete this particular branch of the subject, the day boy houses were re-named Welldon House and Smythe House, to bring them more into line with the rest of the school houses.

Mention of the day boys suggests a reference to the growth of Tonbridge town, though the subject is really outside our compass. The reader may refer to A. H. Neve's excellent little book, *The Tonbridge of Yesterday*.

In Sir Andrew Judde's day Tonbridge was not what we should reckon a town at all. It had probably no more than a few hundred inhabitants. The beginnings of growth may be traced back to about 1740, when the Medway was first canalized and provided with locks. In those days of bad roads and no railways water was the principal means of transporting heavy goods, and Tonbridge became a terminus to which goods were brought for transfer to water and from which imports by water radiated out over the adjoining parts of Kent and Sussex. Coal came to Tonbridge by Medway right down to 1914, and the name of the Medway Coal Company still commemorates this fact. After the opening of the railway in 1842 Tonbridge grew apace, and the population before the end of Dr. Welldon's time had already reached 6,000. To-day it is something like 18,000. Districts likely to house the parents of day boys, such as Dry Hill Park and the Hadlow Road south of Yardley Park corner, reveal by their architecture their Victorian origin. Many day boys came in from outside Tonbridge, more particularly from Tunbridge Wells.

In 1898 Mr. Bickmore, an assistant master at the school, founded the preparatory school at Yardley Court which is now carried on by his sons. It is entirely independent of the old school, but needless to say the two schools have each gladly contributed to the welfare of the other. The foundation of Yardley Court helped to solve the problem of the age for admission to Tonbridge school.

Here is a curious item from Dr. Wood's headmastership. In 1893 the Bishop of Dover, who came to preach to the school, was so much struck by the quality of the chapel choir that he secured for it an invitation (which was accepted) to give a performance of the oratorio 'Christ and His Soldiers', by John Farmer, in Canterbury cathedral. The *Tonbridgian* says that Dr. Brewer, the music master, played the cathedral organ 'we need hardly say, magnificently and made

> *The thunder music, rolling, shake*
> *The prophets blazoned on the panes'.*

This may well be, for he was afterwards 'congratulated by the Dean on having broken the record in the amount of water used by the hydraulic apparatus'. Brewer composed the tune of the *Carmen Tonbridgiense*, the words of which were written by Earl at about this time, though I have been told by an O.T. of the period that they were actually written by Mrs. Earl, who preferred that her husband should take the responsibility for them. Afterwards he became organist of Gloucester Cathedral and was for many years a mainstay of the famous 'Three Choirs' Festival'.

Music and cricket were both at a high level in that year. Records of victorious seasons at cricket and football and the performances of outstanding individuals are outside the scope of this book. 'The match—we lose and win it again', says a school song of another school; such triumphs are properly as ephemeral as they are enthralling. But we may mention that the article on 'Public School Cricket in 1893' in Wisden's Almanac estimated that the Tonbridge XI was one of the three best of the year. There have of course been several Tonbridge elevens and fifteens in more recent years that have deserved, and very likely received, similar testimonials from the impartial annalists of sport.

Mr. Goggs has already been mentioned more than once in these pages. In 1896 he retired from the staff after thirty-four years' service as a teacher of mathematics, but he came to be famous less for his mathematics than his longevity. Living on until 1931 in his little house in Dry Hill Park Road, attending all school matches, and to the last officiating as 'referee' (whatever exactly that may have meant) at the Athletic Sports, he was indeed a link with the past. He was a man of magnificent physique, and with his big white beard he looked rather as W. G. Grace might have looked, one imagines, had he lived to an equal age. There are many stories told of Goggs in his old age, but those who knew him well know them, and those who did not will, alas! not feel interested. As master and 'past-master' he was with us for sixty-nine years and died at the age of ninety-five, bequeathing money both for the prizes that bear his name and for the cricket scoring board on the Head.

In 1898 Dr. Wood was appointed to succeed Dr. Welldon at Harrow, and left at the end of the year. Both men were in different ways 'Tonbridgians' though neither was educated at the school, for Dr. Welldon was the son of Edward Welldon, once house-master of Judde House. Presumably Dr. Welldon of Harrow was born in Old Judde. Dr. Wood appears to have been the only headmaster of Tonbridge except Horne (1640-9) and Goad (1660-2) to go on to the headmastership of another school. The majority of his predecessors had, like Welldon for example, taken up work as clergymen in country parishes.

One labour of love belonging to the period covered by this chapter should not pass unnoticed by a historian of the school, namely, the compilation of the first School Register, recording all available and relevant information about every member of the school from 1820 onwards. The editor was W. O. Hughes-Hughes, O.T. He secured the cordial co-operation of the Governors, who placed at his disposal their complete record of admissions since 1820, in all 2,800 names. Having copied these he got to work in the British Museum Library and 'commenced operations by calling for all the Clergy Lists from 1820 onwards. . . . Having exhausted the Clergy Lists', he writes, 'I treated in the same manner the Army, Navy, Medical, Colonial, Law, Civil Service, etc., lists. . . . Then I printed a list of all the O.T.'s I had failed to trace by these means and sent it to all whom I had traced.' Mr. Hughes-Hughes, who was on the staff at the time, used to go up to London to work on the Register every half-holiday afternoon. At the end of it all he was twenty pounds out of pocket as more than fifty of those who had applied for the book refrained from paying for it. These facts were recorded in the *Tonbridgian* on the occasion of the issue of a second edition of the Register bringing it up to date in 1893.

In 1935 Mr. W. G. Hart extended research much further back in his *Tonbridge School Register*, 1553 *to* 1820.

VII. DR. TANCOCK AND MR. LOWRY
(1899-1922)

Dr. Wood's successor was Dr. Tancock (1899-1906). He had been headmaster of Rossall for ten years but had retired in 1896 owing to a breakdown of health. When he accepted the Tonbridge appointment he seemed to have made a complete recovery, but he was not a strong man and he was one of those devoted servants of whatever institution they may be called on to serve who do not, and temperamentally cannot, spare themselves. In 1906 his health again collapsed and he retired, more or less an invalid for the rest of his life. Dr. Tancock, his predecessor and his successor all died within a few months of one another in 1922-3. Numbers fell in Tancock's first years, owing perhaps to the foundation of Yardley Court preparatory school, which absorbed most of the juniors, but recovered, and when he left there were just over 400 boys in the school. In quality of achievement the school never stood higher. Ten entrance scholarships or exhibitions to Oxford and Cambridge colleges were won in 1902-3, twelve in 1903-4, and in 1903 the school won the Ashburton Shield for the first time. The Governors presented to the school a small bronze replica of the shield in honour of the occasion.

The winning of this shooting trophy, competed for by all the public schools of England, is evidence of the progress of the rifle corps, which then contained 250 members, about two-thirds of the school. In 1907, as an item in Haldane's army reforms, the corps became an O.T.C. and was more closely linked up with the army organization. As a result it changed its uniform from red to khaki, with disastrous consequences for the School Corps song 'In Camp', the chorus of which ran

Then shout hurrah! for the gallant lads in red
Who serve their King at Aldershot as well as on the Head.

Those who are amused by such trifles will find, in an old issue of the *Tonbridgian*, a number of attempts to provide a new chorus of the right 'colour'. Perhaps the song died of its emendations; it has certainly long since disappeared.

The growth in the numbers and the popularity of the corps was, of course, due to the South African War which occupied the last fifteen months of the old century and the first sixteen months of the new one. The relief of Mafeking, in the summer term of 1900, was celebrated with the same riotous enthusiasm at Tonbridge as elsewhere. News of the event arrived about 9 p.m., and 'Though, of course, discipline prevented the school from taking any part in the nocturnal festivities, there was little sleep for anyone, and the houses re-echoed with vociferous cheers till an early hour in the morning. On Saturday morning there was a general rush down town to secure flags and bunting, and by half-past eight there was scarce a boy to be seen without some emblem of patriotic enthusiasm. Soon after, or rather during, breakfast time, Parkside could be seen crowded on a brake and proceeding round the park, escorted on every side by a cavalcade of bicycles, and cheering lustily the while. They were soon joined by the rest of the school'. It sounds a bit hysterical, but it could be matched, and surpassed, by the goings-on in some other schools. No event in the Great Wars of 1914-18 and 1939-45 was celebrated in this hectic fashion, for the nation's outlook on war, even in its brightest moments, had become more adult and more sombre.

Four days after the fall of Mafeking Tonbridge had a celebration all to itself, namely, the laying of the foundation stone of the new chapel. A photograph of the event shows that the ceremony was performed in pouring rain. Two years later, in May 1902, the new chapel completed in one sense yet incomplete in another, for the ante-chapel was not added until seven years later, was consecrated by the Archbishop of Canterbury, assisted by Bishop Welldon, formerly headmaster of Harrow, and three O.T. bishops, Ridgeway of Kensington, Hoare of Victoria, and Wilson of Melanesia. The Governors provided the fabric but left to voluntary subscription the decoration of the building. The architect was Mr. Campbell Jones.

It is unnecessary to describe the chapel in detail for it will be familiar to most readers of this book. But not all who attend its services are aware of the high quality of its stained glass windows. The following account of them is from the guide book, *Kent*, in 'The King's England' series, and was written by one who, so far as we know, had no personal connexion with the school. 'It is for its glass that this chapel will be most remembered. It has some of the famous windows that are the glory of many modern churches and of many old ones, the work of Christopher Whall and of his son, or of Veronica his daughter. We have come across them all over the country (especially in Gloucester Cathedral) and they are an inspiration and delight. The idea of the east window is the glory of the coming of Christ into the world. We see him in the manger, with the kings, shepherds and angels in adoration. . . . There is Michael, holding out his hand to the boys who are coming on, and to the pilgrim on his journey; there is Gabriel, turning to the defeated and discouraged; and above all there is Gloria in Excelsis and on earth Peace.

'The whole group of these Christopher Whall windows is magnificent. In the sanctuary are two windows symbolical of Judgment, an angel in armour with a flaming sword standing by the Recording Angel, and an angel in rich soft clothing holding the palm of victory. Another window has the life of St. Andrew, with four panels from the life of Christ; another has three lancets filled with scenes from the life of St. Margaret of Scotland, and the memorial window for Tonbridge boys who fell in South Africa is filled with the heroism of our own St.

George, and has a shield on which we noticed (we think for the first time in a window) the White Horse of Kent.

'There are also three windows in this chapel by Miss Lilian Pocock, all finely designed and nobly carried out. One has the story of St. Augustine with the saint as the central figure, the scene in Rome market-place where Pope Gregory met the English slave boys, the baptism of Ethelbert in the font at St. Martin's, and the landing of St. Augustine at Ebbsfleet. A St. Denis window shows the saint with the lilies of France in one hand and his banner in the other; smaller scenes show him preaching by the Seine and his martyrdom, with wolves waiting in the snow. The third of Miss Pocock's windows is a brilliant St. Christopher carrying the child across the swirling waters. The best modern building for miles around is this.'

Another excellent feature of the chapel is its fine organ. The building is good, acoustically, for music, but, as many preachers and their listeners know, very difficult for the speaking voice.

In Dr. Tancock's time rowing at last achieved a permanent establishment. Boys who took up rowing had for some years previously been allowed to use the facilities of the town rowing club, but this was not enough. In 1904 the School Boat Club was established and its own boat house built. There is no sport in which such a large number of masters is required for the coaching of a comparatively small number of boys, and nobly has the staff ever since responded to this as to so many other calls to sacrifice what might be regarded as their spare time in the service of the school. A narrow winding river makes eights impossible, but the school four has twice won the public schools' cup at Marlow regatta.

It was in these years, too, that the cross-country race, the Cras, took its present form. Previously it had been a paper-chase of uncertain but formidable dimensions, sometimes extending to One Tree Hill and back. One of the great Tonbridge family of the Nottidges, who was in the school from 1845 to 1854, wrote: 'As I generally ran as "hare" the details of the paper chase did not come under my view. I remember

P. G. Skipwith and I ran as "hares" towards Sevenoaks once, when we were mistaken for two sailors escaped from Maidstone Gaol, for whose capture a reward had been offered, and a policeman in a cart raised the whole countryside on us and we were caught. It all ended in a jollification in a "public" the other side of Hildenborough.' Once again the old days seem to show an advantage over our decorously organized modern times.

In the summer of 1903 the Headmaster's Conference, which meets annually at the school of one of its members, assembled at Tonbridge, and two items in its printed agenda are of interest: (i) a resolution advocating the establishment of a common entrance examination for all public schools—in those days each school had its own examination conducted on its own premises, an obviously inconvenient system which, however, enabled the masters to inspect the candidates as well as their work; (ii) a resolution advocating the abolition of Euclid's Elements in favour of geometry of the modern type.

The breakdown of Dr. Tancock's health created an interregnum in the headmastership, and the duties of the post were entrusted for the next two terms to the Rev. Arthur Lucas, senior assistant master and chaplain. Lucas had joined the staff in 1878 and retired in 1909, a devoted and enterprising servant of the school. In days when masters as a rule left the games to look after themselves Lucas had played regularly on the Head and coached at the nets. He presented the first of the now almost too numerous house challenge cups, that for cricket. In his early days he had taken a Tonbridge cricket eleven to play a series of matches in Holland during the summer holidays. He had started the school mission in St. Pancras, acting as its secretary and treasurer for twenty-five years and making up the annual deficit, it was rumoured, from his own pocket. The establishment of the sanatorium was also very largely his work, and both he and Mrs. Lucas made it one of their special interests. Such a career was fittingly crowned by a brief 'regency' which Lucas is believed to have thoroughly enjoyed. He was succeeded at Parkside by R. L. Aston, an Old Boy of the school and a rugger international, who coached a long succession of powerful fifteens.

In succession to Dr. Tancock the Governors appointed Mr. Charles Lowry (1907-22), an Old Etonian, who had been an assistant master at Eton and then headmaster of Sedbergh. He was the first lay headmaster, but like his two lay successors he preached at least twice a term at Sunday evening services, and also took the short daily service on Monday mornings. Many will remember his characteristic and often topical prayers composed for these services.

Charles Lowry was a man on whose characteristics all who knew him would be tempted to linger, for there was something peculiarly attractive about him. There is an old Rugby epigram, dating from the brief and disastrous headmastership of Dr. Hayman, seventy years ago, which runs somewhat as follows: 'If the headmaster can neither teach, nor preach, nor organize, then he ought to be either a scholar or a gentleman.' Those who have known many headmasters at close quarters will find amusement in applying the test to those they have known, and seeing whether they score 'distinctions', passes, or failures in each of the five 'subjects'. Probably *no* headmaster would score a distinction in all five, if the tests were applied with appropriate severity; such is the diversity of gifts demanded in these exacting days.

However, let us apply the tests to Lowry. Teacher—agreeable and in the best sense educative, but not much use for examinations. It used to be said that when 'Chas' (as we called him, from his old-fashioned style of signature—Chas. Lowry) undertook to read with the Classical Sixth one of the set books for the summer examinations, W. M. Gordon surreptitiously took the form through the book himself as well, to ensure that they should know something about it. Preacher—good, manly and direct, and full of personality, but without the personality the sermons would have created no great impression. Organizer—in this department Lowry was a mere child. Scholar— an accomplished Classical scholar in the old Etonian tradition, the kind of scholarship which would have appealed to Vicesimus Knox, who ruled over Tonbridge a hundred years before him, a fragrant flower of elegant accomplishment, now trampled under foot by the advancing hosts of studies supposedly more useful. When a bird entered the chapel and built her nest somewhere in the organ, Lowry composed a little Greek ode on the subject. Up to this point the record is not, perhaps, altogether convincing. We pass on to the last test. Gentleman—distinction absolute and unsurpassable. Charles Lowry had the most important of all gifts for headmastership; he was, by nature and without conscious effort, the kind of man that the ordinary boy believes he can understand, and feels impelled to admire, venerate and love. He had his faults and foibles, no doubt, a strong temper not always controlled, a too great readiness to give extra half-holidays; but there was something about him, a kind of nobility, that was of more than common stature. The fact that he was there at all, much more than anything he did, was the measure of Lowry's contribution to Tonbridge. Himself an Eton 'wet bob', the school rowing was one of his special interests. On one occasion, during the race against Winchester, when bicycling along the tow-path in attendance on the crew he had coached, he went right into the river. He emerged roaring with laughter, and the event provoked 'odes' in a variety of languages, both from himself and his more accomplished colleagues. Lowry had one important qualification for a rowing coach—a very powerful voice. All who knew him will remember its use in chapel. If he felt that the singing was getting a bit slack he would suddenly let his voice out, and it out-roared the rest of us as easily as a Wagnerian hero dominates a Wagnerian orchestra.

At the end of Lowry's first year Henry Hilary retired after nearly forty years in the service of the school, having been appointed to the staff by Welldon in 1870. Hilary was a man of really first-rate intellectual powers. He raised the mathematical scholarship of the school to a high level, and turned out a long series of pupils who subsequently won high distinction. He was also a good classical scholar and took up, almost as a hobby, the study of Arabic and other Oriental languages in which he achieved such distinction that he was invited to edit some of the mathematical treatises of ancient Arabic scholars. But he did not feel any inclination to do so. He was a man who might have excelled and won fame in any of several different branches of learning. Being entirely without ambition, he contented himself with the humdrum duties of teaching schoolboys and never asked for more. His portrait, by Tattershall Dodd the younger, hangs in the Masters' Common Room, as also do portraits of E. H. Goggs, G. A. Floyd, H. R. Stokoe and M. A. Buckmaster, painted and presented by the same artist; and there is also a portrait of Mr. Buckmaster by his old pupil, C. K. Hauff, in the Art School. Otherwise assistant masters have to stake their hopes of a visible immortality on the photographic groups, taken about once in every ten years and preserved in an album in the Common Room. They make an interesting study. The first group, dated 1863, shows Dr. Welldon with ten assistants, all but one of them whiskered and five of them in Holy orders. The last group, dated 1945, shows Mr. Whitworth surrounded by a noble army of masters, between thirty and forty of them. The whiskers have gone and only one, the chaplain, is in Holy orders, and—since the war had only just ended—four ladies appear among the staff.

Early in his headmastership Mr. Lowry established the tutorial system, an imitation on a much more modest scale of the most characteristic of all Eton institutions. Every boy, unless he is taking 'special classes' in a weak subject, usually for school certificate purposes, has a tutor, and visits him at his private house once a week in the evening. Only those who are not boarding-house masters act as tutors. The occupations of the tutorial hour are of unlimited diversity, Lowry's only stipulation being that they should not include school work. The main purpose of the system is to give each boy an evening out once a week, away from his boarding-house routine, and an informal friendly contact with another master, usually a young master, in addition to his house-master, and there can be little doubt that the tutor system has contributed to foster the spirit of friendliness and co-operation between boys and masters

4. HENRY HILARY, CHIEF MATHEMATICAL
MASTER 1870-1908
from an oil painting by C. Tattershall Dodd, jun.

which characterizes the school. For day boys the system may have less value but, since the day boy house-masters are themselves entitled to take 'pupils', it affords them a means of getting to know the boys for whom as house-masters they are responsible. The inclusion of the day boys in the system, even at some inconvenience to themselves if they do not live close to the school, also conforms to the essential principle that day boys shall, as far as possible, undergo exactly the same routine as boarders. It is largely through the observance of this principle that the day boys have become an integral and highly respected section of the school.

Somewhere about the same time Lowry abolished the gowns hitherto worn by scholars and the surplices of the choir. Gowns are now worn only by School Prepostors when reading the lessons in chapel. As for the surplices they remained on their pegs in the vestry for years, ten or fifteen years, after their disuse, a hideous waste of ecclesiastical *lingerie*. Then one suddenly observed that they had disappeared. Perhaps they had gone to cover the nakedness of some deserving choir elsewhere.

In 1910 the new sanatorium was opened. 'The death of King Edward made it necessary to abandon the ceremony of opening the new sanatorium. The school were allowed to go over it for one day and, on the next, a patient was moved in from Old Judde.' Thus the *Tonbridgian*. The new 'San' was of course an immense improvement on the make-shift arrangements in Old Judde. Indeed even to-day, after thirty years' service, it seems as good as new and incapable of improvement. It generally surpasses, we understand, the expectations of those who are taken to inspect it. As for Old Judde it served very miscellaneous purposes for the next sixteen years, but its old dining-hall was used to provide mid-day dinner for those day boys who could not get home in the middle of the school day.

The very last 'pre-war' event in Tonbridge history was the playing of the first match at Lords against Clifton. The famous thirteen days, which began with Austria's ultimatum to Serbia and ended with Great Britain's ultimatum to Germany on behalf of Belgian neutrality, were already in progress, and within a week of the match, the 'First Great War', as perhaps we shall come to call it, had begun.

It is interesting to study in the *Tonbridgians* of 1914-16, the very gradual impact of the war upon the life of the school. We turn pages and pages of war news—lists of O.T.'s serving, obituary notices of the fallen, but of the school under war conditions, how the war affected the daily life of the school, one gets little idea, probably because in the first year or two the normal life was not much affected. The O.T.C. of course expanded and became practically conterminous with the school itself; the now normal Monday morning parades in place of the last hour of school work were instituted and Wednesday half-holidays were often devoted to field operations. For some months in 1914 the armoury was guarded day and night by members of the corps, we are told. In the summer holidays of 1916 the O.C. with great enterprise organized an O.T.C. camp at Penshurst, inviting contingents from other schools. About 600 cadets assembled, and 'before the other schools arrived every bit of canvas was put up by Tonbridge cadets themselves, to say nothing of a wonderful erection for holding our water supplies'.

In March 1916 we read of two war novelties that had in fact come to stay, the former for over twenty years and the latter for ever—daily P.T. and 'the Pound'. The latter had hitherto been what its name implies, a place to which lost books were taken for reclamation. Henceforth, owing to the demand for economy, it began to buy school-books and issue them on loan as it now does.

Very different is the picture presented by the *Tonbridgians* of 1917-18. By that time the school, like other civilian institutions, had become entangled in the whirlpool of war. For example, one who signs himself 'Anti-German' writes to say that the school tuck shop ought to be closed at once. 'The majority of the houses are on rations; yet how can they say that they are on rations if they privately indulge in large quantities of unnecessary food?' The editors' response seems to be to print the slogan 'Eat less bread' in larger and blacker letters than can be found anywhere else in the columns of the paper from 1858 to the present day.

In May 1917 we learn that 'later on in the term the school is going out in detachments to work on the land, especially in the hay fields'. In November we read that 'the school has been reaping the fruits of its agricultural labours, and our hearty thanks are due . . . excellent vegetables'. Contingents from the school went harvesting during the summer holidays of 1917 in Yorkshire and Essex, and in 1918 had 'two very successful harvest camps at Chilmark near Salisbury', run by members of the staff. It is interesting that during the war years the *Tonbridgian* doubled its circulation among Old Boys.

Yet much of course went on as before, and the standards maintained in scholarship, cricket and football results were, as it happened, well above the average.

Rivington's *History* contains a section on Tonbridge during the war, contributed by one who was on the staff at the time. A quotation from it will supplement what we have already recorded. 'Mingled with our normal activities were many novelties. Munitions were made in the workshops at an early date. On the "Fifty" the space now occupied by the hard tennis courts was robbed of its excellent turf and devoted to the cultivation of the all-important potato and other vegetables. Boys might be seen there and on Martin's and Mr. Fleming's fields wielding the spade and the hoe with zealous, if not very expert, patriotism. . . . At other times neighbouring farmers drew upon the school to make good the shortage of farm hands. . . .

'Food is never a dull subject at school, and during the war it became more engrossing. The "Grubber" inevitably had less to offer. Rations made house-keeping a nightmare, and housemasters grew pale with the effort of calculating how much "offal", as the Food Controller unkindly called it, might be added to the weekly allowance of meat, or what would happen if a boy's parents did not send back his butter card.

'A more pleasant feature of this time was the frequent appearance of Old Tonbridgians in uniform. . . . Among these visitors airmen were the most tantalizing. It became apparently a point of honour with O.T. flying officers to swoop down upon the school in an aeroplane, fly low over School House or the chapel roof, and circle round with amazing stunts before they departed on their business. More than one saluted us with Verey lights. Such visitors often passed on unknown; but sometimes they came so low, looking over the side, that they could be recognized, and once at least a boy on the London Road ground was able to greet his brother in the sky. . . . One officer landed so forcibly on Martin's that he rushed through the hedge into the hop field opposite Judde House. The aeroplane was hauled back into the school grounds and faithfully protected at nights by guards from the O.T.C. till it was dismantled by mechanics and carried away in a lorry. The propeller-boss still hangs in the bottom corridor of the New Buildings as a memento of the incident.'

And so on to the first Armistice Day. 'The news', says the *Tonbridgian*, 'arrived at about 11.15 and couriers sped to the class-rooms to announce it. All plans had already been formulated. The Corps fell in on the "Quad", and an open-air service was held. It was most impressive, and the noise of church bells, engine whistles, and rifle shots only served to heighten its impressiveness. . . . After lunch the Corps fell in again and took part in a procession through the town. Speeches were delivered by Mr. Lowry and by the Chairman of the Urban District Council, in the middle of the town.' At five o'clock there was a lecture and at 7.30 an impromptu sing-song.

Some time before November of a year later someone in a letter to the Press suggested the idea of the two-minutes' silence as an annual commemoration of the event, and at that hour on 11th November 1919 the school assembled, in mufti, in front of the Old School Buildings. I happened to be standing next to Mr. Lowry and Mr. Gordon on that occasion, and heard one of them remark to the other, 'We shall never get this properly arranged unless we bring the boys on by word of command'; and the other said, 'In that case they had better be in uniform.' Thus it was done in 1920. A few years later Armistice Day fell on a Sunday, and the two minutes' silence was taken as the central point of a special service. Some of us considered that this was more appropriate than the military parade, and the next year, though a week-day, the two minutes' silence was again taken in chapel. Thereupon many in the town expressed regret, for the school ceremonial in the open air, adjoining the High Street, with its National Anthem and Last Post, had become for many living in the northern half of the town the local equivalent of the ceremonial at the Cenotaph in Westminster. So a compromise was adopted. The chapel service was maintained but preceded, instead of including, the two minutes' silence which was held, as before, in front of the school.

In the term preceding the outbreak of the war numbers stood at 413, and had dropped to 374 in 1916. Thereafter they rose and continued to rise steadily. In the first summer term after the armistice they stood at 459, surpassing previous records, and in 1926, four years after Mr. Lowry had gone, they reached 495. These numbers merely illustrate a 'curve' that was common to the public schools as a whole. Almost every school experienced a falling off in the first half of the war that was more than compensated by a rise in the second half, which continued through most of the first decade of peace. Some schools built new boarding-houses. Entirely new schools, such as Stowe and Canford, were started and filled rapidly. Many new boarding preparatory schools flourished. Besides this many new girls' boarding schools, such as Benenden and Bedgebury, to mention only our nearest neighbours, established themselves in country houses which their owners could no longer afford to inhabit. If statistics were to be compiled they would show that the total population of boarding schools of all sorts was not only greater in the decade 1920-30, but markedly greater than in any previous period. The number of births was already declining, but it had not yet had time to affect the school-age population, which was more or less stationary. The cause of this boom in boarding schools is a rather intricate subject which we cannot here explore.

Tonbridge met the increase in its boarder numbers (the

number of day boys being more or less a fixture) by erecting an 'army hut' containing three class-rooms behind the chapel, and by the 'sleeping out' system. Five junior boys from each house were boarded out for sleeping and changing accommodation, but not for meals, with various married non-housemasters. The system was obviously a temporary expedient but it served its purpose and did no harm. The small boys probably rather enjoyed it, for they generally got very comfortable quarters. It also put a little easy money in the pockets of a very deserving class, the married non-housemasters.

Lowry was one of those on whom the deaths in battle of his old pupils, Etonians, Sedberghians, and Tonbridgians, pressed with an almost unbearable strain. In 1917 his health broke down, and he was ordered a complete rest. Many thought he would not return, and Mr. Earl was appointed acting-headmaster. But Lowry recovered and returned, and Earl shortly afterwards retired after thirty-four years' service. His work as the founder of the science side has already been mentioned. He was an inspiring teacher and a good organizer; he made a brilliant success of his own department, but he also contributed to the school life in other ways. He and Mrs. Earl had more contacts than schoolmasters generally have with the wider world of contemporary literature and art. Many brilliant persons with well-known names came down to enjoy their hospitality at Ferox Hall, and 'Old Ferocians' of Earl's day remember with gratitude the contacts with a wider culture than that of mere scholasticism, which when senior boys they were privileged to share.

In Lowry's later years he entrusted more and more of the internal management of the school to the head of his classical side, Walter Maxwell Gordon. No account of Tonbridge would be complete without some estimate of that remarkable man.

I was once privileged to travel in the same railway carriage with Dr. Lyttelton, headmaster of Eton, and another of the elder statesmen of the profession. I remember Lyttelton saying, 'I wonder what boys talk about in these days. When I was a boy, so far as I can remember, we spent a good deal of time

5. CHARLES LOWRY, HEADMASTER
1907-22
from an oil painting by A. Spence Watson

talkin' about the masters; and, my word, there were some masters worth talkin' about in those days.' Gordon was of that order—a tremendous personality. When old members of the Classical Upper Sixth, or of Judde House, encountered one another, the conversation would sooner or later come round to Gordon. He was not a man of wide intellectual interests, but he was in his own way a wonderful teacher. He was as successful as any crammer could be in winning scholarships both for those who did, and those who did not, deserve them, and he was as continuously entertaining in school as any hero of the stage. One mark of his forceful pedagogy was deservedly famous. He had a peculiarly neat handwriting, which he taught and enforced upon every boy in his form and his house. Those who do not know this will hardly believe it, but every member of the Upper Sixth in the years 1919-23 wrote a more or less faithful replica of the Gordonian hand. I know this, for I had their English work. Of the house I cannot speak, but I believe it was the same there. Certainly they all had writing lessons.

When Lowry retired Gordon stood for the headmastership, and when it was known that he was one of the three select candidates, excitement ran high, and it is creditable to Gordon that a majority of the staff, as it seemed, desired his appointment. The Governors decided otherwise, and there are certainly obvious and strong arguments in favour of choosing the 'new broom' from outside the staff. A year later he accepted the headmastership of Wrekin College.

In February 1922 Lowry's health broke down completely. Another interregnum, the third in eighteen years, was inevitable, and Mr. Stokoe took charge for a term and a half. Henry Stokoe had joined the staff in 1890 and retired at the age of seventy in 1931, having been forty-one years house-master of Park House. His career was one of continuous and unswerving devotion to all the interests of the school. He was, it may be said in no derogatory sense, every inch a schoolmaster, and a man who would take infinite pains over tasks that others might shirk as tedious. In a *Tonbridgian* of his first year appear the words 'Cheques should be made payable to H. R. Stokoe, Esq.,

Park House', and so it always was thereafter. His most arduous labour of love was the volume *Tonbridge School and the Great War*, probably the most complete record compiled for any school, as it gave details of the war careers not only of all who fell, but of all who served. In this record we find that, at the outbreak of the war, 234 O.T.'s held commissions on the active lists of the navy and army, and 124 were in the reserve and territorial forces. The total number of those who eventually served was 2,382 and 21 masters. The Roll of Honour includes the names of 415 O.T.'s and 3 masters. Of these Mr. Stokoe collected and reproduced the photographs of 401. The photographs themselves are hung on the walls of the ground-floor corridor of the New Buildings.

Mr. Stokoe's principal class-room interest was grammatical analysis, and after his retirement he published what is probably the completest textbook on the subject in existence.

A few of the assistant masters from William McGill onwards have found their way into the narrative and one or two more will make openings for themselves in the next chapter. Nothing could be more inappropriate than a catalogue of these servants of the school who have served it certainly without any idea of getting their names into 'history', but for the reader's sake rather than for theirs it may be as well to take a look round and so collect a few more; and for this purpose let us use the photographic group of the staff taken in 1919 immediately after the first Great War. There is Charles Lowry seated in the middle of the front row, not looking his very noble best, looking in fact rather bored and tired. Also in occupation of seats of seniority are Stokoe, Buckmaster and Aston, already mentioned and H. O. Whitby, first house-master of Judde House after its removal from 'the city' to 'the suburbs', a most charming man and a notable cricketer. Was he not a member of the only Oxford eleven that ever beat the Australians? I hope I am right in saying so. Then there is H. C. Stewart, just about to retire from the control of the school music; also a man of great personal charm and very varied athletic accomplishment. He rowed at Oxford, played cricket for Kent, played for something else at association football and was an outstandingly skilful performer on the ice. Next to him one sees the bald head and white moustache of G. A. Floyd, who preferred not to undertake the burdens of house-mastering but was for many years a very thorough teacher of fifth-form classics. Floyd was one of those schoolmasters who are associated with certain stereotyped jokes which always come off even when one knows they are coming. If, when taking the ages of his form at the beginning of the term, he came to a boy of exceptional maturity he would ask, without looking up from his mark book, 'Married or single?' But perhaps his chief interest was in his rose garden from which he won many prizes.

Standing behind are Seargent, Gordon, Arnold and Dodd, all of them introduced elsewhere; also C. H. Crofts, an O.T. and for many years house-master of Manor House. Crofts was an enthusiast for the navy and persuaded practically the whole school to become members of the Navy League. The Tonbridge branch of the Navy League for many years organized lectures not only on naval subjects but on anything else that came handy. Indeed for many years there were two sorts of lectures provided in the winter terms, 'School lectures' which were compulsory and 'Navy League lectures' which were voluntary, and the latter were considered to be the better of the two, either because they were better or because they were voluntary.

In the obscurer quarters of the group one detects certain slim and youthful figures who, when no longer youthful and in some cases no longer slim, remained with us until very recent times. Three indeed are still with us at the time (1946) when these words are being written.

VIII. RECENT YEARS (1922-46)

As a history of a school approaches the present day the writer finds difficulty in maintaining the interest of his work—or, if you prefer, he grows duller than ever. Recent events are too obvious and familiar to his readers; they lack the charms of oddity or romance. If he is conscientiously thorough he has an uncomfortable feeling that he is encroaching on the province of the school prospectus. That handsomely produced and illustrated brochure is freely distributed to all who ask for it, and it sets forth, in language studiously impersonal but, it is hoped, persuasive, all that the school has to offer in the way of organization and equipment. The present writer does not intend to enter into competition with the prospectus, nor does he feel equal to surmounting the handicaps which the last laps of his long journey impose upon him. The most he can promise is that, though he may be dull, he will be reasonably brief.

In succession to Mr. Lowry the Governors appointed as headmaster Mr. H. N. P. Sloman (1922-39). Educated at Rugby, he had been successively an assistant master at Radley, headmaster of a big day school in Sydney, Australia, and after that for a few terms head of the modern side at Rugby. He had seen active service in the war and had been awarded the Military Cross. He was our first headmaster to see active service since Christopher Wase (1662-68) who had served in the Spanish army against France when an exile from England during the Commonwealth.

124

Each headmaster brings to his task his own gifts, and no two the same. Harold Sloman was one of the most intellectually gifted of all our headmasters, and probably none of his predecessors had as wide a range of accomplishment. An expert classical scholar, he was also equipped to take sixth form work in French and German. At the age of fifty he still retained the intellectual inquisitiveness of the best sort of undergraduate, and as a true Athenian he always desired to hear some new thing. Like all the best teachers he was always learning. Teaching was, no doubt, the part of his work that he enjoyed most. He was also one of the kindest and most considerate of men, to boys and masters alike. There have been modern headmasters (not in Tonbridge) who have found what psychologists call 'compensation' for their benevolence to the boys by grinding the faces of their assistant masters. But Mr. Sloman was kind-hearted by nature. It was characteristic of him that he liked to be regarded, and was regarded, as a member of his own Masters' Common Room, where he usually spent the mid-morning break solving, with continuous assistance from some and occasional interjections from others, the *Times* crossword puzzle. Such a man leaves agreeable memories behind him.

When he retired the editors of the *Tonbridgian* wrote of him: 'His reign was distinguished by a wide and tolerant humanity, by a charity of outlook which seldom and reluctantly condemned, which chose to guide and lead rather than to order and drive, which abhorred the idea of a headmaster as "a beast but a just beast", supplanting it by an unaffected and friendly intercourse with all whom he met, boys and masters alike.'

During the latter years of his headmastership Mr. Sloman's management of the school came in for criticism. The fact is so well known to those interested in the school that it would be cowardice in a historian to ignore the fact, and what I have to say about it I say as one who values his personal friendship. A headmaster's business is of two kinds, which we may classify as 'domestic affairs' and 'foreign policy'. Domestic affairs includes his handling of his boys and masters. Foreign policy includes his relationships with the governors, the parents, the headmasters of preparatory schools and the Old Boys. It is on a head-master's domestic policy that the day by day and term by term welfare of his school depends, but it is largely by his foreign policy that he makes the school's reputation, and it was in his foreign policy that Mr. Sloman was, in his later years, some-what unsuccessful, and by reason of his defective foreign policy the school's reputation declined during the last years of his headmastership. There is no harm in being frank about this now, seeing that its reputation has since completely recovered. Mr. Whitworth has told some of us that after he had accepted the headmastership as Mr. Sloman's successor he was from several quarters warned that he would find 'an awful atmosphere of slackness'. Actually, he was agreeably and completely sur-prised. There were some things he wanted to alter—what new headmaster does not find such?—but in the main he found that he had taken over a healthy and vigorous school. I might put it this way. A parent who sent his boy to Tonbridge in 1934 for the last five years of Mr. Sloman's headmastership got just about as good value, morally and intellectually, for his money as the parent who sent his boy in 1939 for the first five years of Mr. Whitworth's headmastership, or at any other date you like to choose for any other five years of the school's history.

One of Mr. Sloman's first actions was to introduce the School Leaving Certificate Examination for the fifth forms, a measure which certainly did not diminish the industriousness of the average boy.

One of the results of lay headmasterships was to give more independence and significance than hitherto to the position of the chaplain. This position was held during the middle years of Mr. Sloman's headmastership by the Rev. S. H. Clarke, who accepted a headmastership in Johannesburg in 1934. Sydney Clarke was an Anglo-Catholic of what seemed by Ton-bridge standards an extreme type. All his colleagues did not see eye to eye with him, for the traditions of the school since Dr. Welldon's day had been definitely Evangelical, but no one could fail to respect his unflagging devotion to his work. He made religion a reality to many boys who would have accepted the older type of churchmanship as a mere school routine, and he connected the school up more closely than before with the Tonbridge club in St. Pancras, taking parties of boys there for week-ends and organizing, with the help of lay colleagues, brief camps for the club boys at Tonbridge, not only after the end of the summer term but during the Whitsun week-end also. Sydney Clarke had a tremendous power of work. He might be described in the terms of Mrs. Malaprop's definition of Cerberus, as 'three gentlemen at once', for he was also senior mathematical master, and devoted his afternoons to coaching small-boy cricket or refereeing at rugger. His well-stocked bookshelves were a lending library for all his pupils and many others; and he found, as most find who indulge in this form of good works, that 'lending' sometimes proved a 'terminological inexactitude'. One of his old pupils, both in mathematics and in churchmanship, is now his successor.

In October 1925 the school war memorial was dedicated by Russell Wakefield, Bishop of Birmingham, and unveiled by General Ironside, both of them Old Boys of the school. The idea of the memorial is a 'gateway of remembrance' through which the whole school passes every day on its way from the ante-chapel into the choir of the chapel. At the same time the *Tonbridgian* published a special illustrated chapel supplement, containing detailed descriptions not only of the war memorial but of all the windows and other decorations. It is bound up with the *Tonbridgians* of that year in the library and is well worth consulting by all who desire an intelligent appreciation of the place in which they worship.

The building plans of the last years of the nineteenth century had put a rather severe strain on the endowment, but shortly after the opening of the new century the income of the Judde foundation was greatly increased by the falling in of some long leases, and the Governors were able to undertake extensive schemes for the improvement of the buildings of both the schools in Tonbridge for which they were now responsible as Sir Andrew Judde's trustees. The new chapel and the new sanatorium, both of them very large items of expenditure, have already been mentioned as they fell within Mr. Lowry's pre-war years. In 1927 the new Music School was built and opened, and music for the first time received accommodation worthy of a great public school. 'No more', write the editors of the *Tonbridgian* with something more than their usual brilliance, 'will the strains of cornet, flute, harp, saxophone and psaltery mingle with the effluvia produced by the untiring efforts of our eminent scientists; no longer shall we be forced on alternate Tuesdays to have P.T. punctuated by the piercing shrieks of tortured trebles and aggressive altos, whose chief aim in life appears to be that of Flecker's immortal pilgrims who endeavoured to go always a little higher (or have we misquoted?). For hard by the horrid hut'—the Army hut, soon to be demolished—'stands a beautiful mansion, complete with pleasure gardens and fire escapes, where those who wish may scrape the fiddle or twang the harp in a padded cell.'

This quotation is a reminder that at about this date there appeared and continued for two years a private venture magazine, entirely produced by boys and entitled *Myops*. Such magazines appear from time to time in all schools, but *Myops* was of unusual quality, and did not rely for its circulation on rather cheap wit, as such productions often do. The moving spirit of it—why should he not be named?—was Denis Crofton, now in the Indian Civil Service.

At about the same time as the building of the Music School the Governors undertook the improvement, sometimes by very extensive additions, of every one of the seven boarding-houses. Though the houses were enlarged the numbers within were not increased; in fact, they were diminished by the abolition of the 'sleeping out' system. Henceforth every house, including the day boy houses, held 50, except the headmaster's which held 70. This fixed the maximum of the school at 470, and to that figure it was reduced, by deliberate curtailment of entries in the course of the next few years. Every one of the school houses has its own style of architecture, and their enlargement set the architect, Mr. Campbell Jones, some very pretty problems which he solved, we think, extremely successfully.

The enlargement of the boarding-houses was due, it appears, to some adverse criticism in the report following the Board of Education inspection of the school in 1925. These inspections of public schools, which began in the early years of the present century and are held about once every ten years, have proved very salutary. They do not often tell an efficient headmaster anything he does not know already but they strengthen his hands, for the purpose of getting things done, as in the example just given. Or again, the inspectors may inform a headmaster that Mr. X is entirely incapable of keeping order and consequently of imparting such knowledge as he possesses. The headmaster will have been for a long time painfully aware of this fact but his kindly disposition may have inhibited his sense of duty. The inspectors tilt the balance in favour of the latter virtue, and Mr. X disappears, to the great advantage of the school and possibly also of Mr. X, who may find a sphere of greater usefulness elsewhere. Much is said, and rightly, of the danger of an excessive interference by the State and its minions with the independence of the public schools, but the degree of interference involved in a decennial inspection, followed by a report which is purely advisory in character, is open to no objection and has, on the contrary, proved its value.

At about the same time—the building activities of the years 1925-30 were really remarkable—there occurred a complicated rearrangement of teaching accommodation, the main features of which are perhaps just worth recording. 'Old Judde' was given a new 'inside', consisting of eight excellent classrooms. This entailed the exile from 'Old Judde' of (i) the day boys who were given a dining-hall and changing room in Dry Hill House; (ii) most of the music teaching, which migrated to the new Music School; (iii) the 'Pound', i.e. the store of loanable school textbooks, which migrated to the two small class-rooms (one of them Mr. Stokoe's) at the top of the narrow stone staircase. Below the Pound an office for the headmaster's secretary was established. Then the Army hut was demolished and its classes moved into the central part of the building which to-day has art and biology on its flanks. This building had pre-

viously been the wood workshops, whereas the metal workshops had been in the basement of the 1894 main building.
Both wood and metal workshops were now shifted to a derelict
chapel just outside the school grounds across the Lansdowne
road, and the basement of the main building was dedicated to
mathematics, an occupation which if not more educative is
certainly less noisy than metal workshops.

Two more important buildings belong to the latter years of
Mr. Sloman's reign. First of all, the new squash courts—Tonbridge boys showed their appreciation of these by winning the
public schools squash trophy two years in succession; and last,
the new Art School and Biology Department, opened in November 1936 by H.R.H. the Duke of Kent. The removal of
biology and art from the old Science Buildings made possible
a great improvement in the accommodation provided for
physics and chemistry. When the Science Buildings were
opened in 1887 they were as good as those possessed by any
school and better than most. Even in 1936 they were not inadequate, but the improvements made that year put them once
again in the forefront of progress. It was a fitting culmination of
Mr. Seargent's long career. He had joined the staff in 1901, taken
over the headship of his department from Earl in 1918, and now
retired in 1937. As for Mr. Buckmaster, the exhibition of work
by some of his old pupils, held in his new palatial quarters, was a
reminder of what he has done for artistically gifted boys in many
ways and more particularly in the training of future architects.

One of the outstanding institutions of the inter-war period
was the annual Shakespeare play, performed at the end of the
Christmas term and produced by Mr. Arnold. The first performance was of *Julius Caesar* in 1921 with W. F. Oakeshott,
afterwards headmaster of Winchester, in the part of Antony,
and the last was *Hamlet* in 1939.[1] In the intervening years
nearly all the more famous plays were performed, some of

---

[1] In this performance the part of Polonius was taken by Sidney Keyes who,
three years later, was killed on active service in North Africa. Shortly after his
death his poems were published and won high praise from authoritative critics.
It seems possible that some of his poems will live as a permanent contribution to
the vast heritage of English poetry.

them more than once. The most notable actors produced were undoubtedly T. H. Tilling and H. C. McComas, and the performance of *Lear* with Tilling in the title role and McComas in the part of Cordelia was probably the most distinguished of the series. The war, with its air raids, brought these festivals to an end, and before they could be revived Arnold had gone. On his part they were indeed a labour of love. Rehearsal was meticulously thorough, and every performance bore the stamp of his personality.

It is tempting to linger for a moment on Arnold, for he was one of the most lovable of men. His forty years of service were all passed in Manor House, first as an unofficial assistant house-master and afterwards as house-master himself. Though professionally a scientist his real interests were in literature and art and, being a comparatively wealthy bachelor, he filled Manor House, which in itself provided an admirable setting, with fine old furniture, pictures and glass. To be familiar with his collections was in itself no small contribution to a liberal education. It is curious to recall that, though a British citizen from birth, he was by descent pure German—Arnold Hoffman until he dropped his surname on joining the Army in 1914, and indeed to his friends, masters and boys, he was always Hoffy. There must be many for whom the memory of Hoffy is cogent evidence that *homo Germanicus* cannot be by nature irreclaimable for civilization.

In his earlier Shakespeare productions he received expert assistance from his friend Winifred Ashton, known to the reading public as Clemence Dane. She also wrote the words of our very fine school song, 'Hail and Farewell', set to music by Dr. Thomas Wood, at that time (1921) Director of Music. If it be true that our earlier—and sadly inferior—school song was written by Mrs. Earl we have the curious fact that our two chief school songs were written by women.

The words of 'Hail and Farewell' are not easily procured except in ephemeral concert programmes, so we print them here, noting that the fourth verse is usually omitted in performance.

I*

This is the school of to-morrow: already my haunts deny me.
  I am shut out of the garden, the dusty high road waits
Yet ever again I turn as the milestone years flash by me,
  For a look at the Head and the Fifty, and the School behind her
      gates:
For the hopes of youth are flowers of the field cut down but the field
      remaineth—
          Greeting, Tonbridge, Tonbridge!
          Farewell, Mother of sons!

This is Yesterday's School: years are the bricks that stayed her,
  She has grown old in honour, twenty kings she has known.
Since a schoolboy granted the charter, and a merchant-venturer
      made her,
  Her thousand boys have ventured wherever a wind has blown.
As leaves on the wind they pass and are gone, but the greening tree
      remaineth—
          Greeting, Tonbridge, Tonbridge!
          Farewell, Mother of sons!

This is the School of To-day, she that received and oppressed me,
  Bidding the novi 'cannot' learn from the lips of 'can'.
Serving in turn I ruled. Thus she taught me her lesson and blessed
      me,
  And now saluting speeds me into the world—a man;
For the days of youth are winnowed chaff, but the golden grain
      remaineth—
          Greeting, Tonbridge, Tonbridge!
          Farewell, Mother of sons!

Court or camp or workshop, wherever I chance to meet him
  Elder by thirty summers, boy with a name unknown,
Beggar or prince, it is one—let him speak but the name and I greet
      him—
  'This is my brother, my brother, this is my mother's son'.
Scattered wide are the beads of the chain but the rope of the chain
      remaineth—

Greeting, Tonbridge, Tonbridge!
Farewell, Mother of sons!

This is the School, my school; I am a word in her story:
  Each unto each has given, something is still to give;
For my shame shall be her sorrow, and my gain shall be her glory.
  Though I die and mine own forget me, my name is here—and I
    live.
For teacher and taught touch hands and part, but the School, the
    School remaineth—
      Greeting, Tonbridge, Tonbridge!
      Farewell, Mother of sons!

I am told that Tom Wood was not himself wholly satisfied with
the fine tune he wrote for these words; he felt that it was rather
too complicated. He wanted to write a tune such as the average
unmusical boy would whistle as he went about his daily business. It is rather a difficult tune, for it has to fit a complicated
stanza, but it is a grand tune and we would not have it other
than it is. If all the public schools were to put their best songs,
words and music together, in competition before some judge
who, while educated at no one of these schools, yet understood
the spirit which animates all of them alike, we feel confident that
'Hail and Farewell' would secure a place very high up in the list.

Another admirable annual entertainment, which started
about the same time as the Shakespeare plays and has been
revived after the worst of the 'blitz' was over, is the Skinners'
Day performance, unstaged, of a Gilbert and Sullivan opera.
Those who have not heard unstaged, or concert-room, performances of these works would be surprised to find how much
of their spirit can be preserved in such presentations if the
soloists enter into their parts in the right spirit. We were fortunate in having on the staff from the start of these performances
down to the present day two masters, both of them Old Tonbridgians, who might well have made their fortunes, the one
as a Henry Lytton and the other as a Rutland Barrington, had
they not preferred more humdrum careers.

Another addition to the gaieties of the Tonbridge nation was the institution—or was it a revival?—of an annual dance on the evening of Old Boys' Day in the middle of the summer term. Business, or rather charity, is combined with pleasure, for the substantial proceeds of the sale of tickets are devoted to the Tonbridge Clubs in St. Pancras.

We have also to record a subtraction from our gaieties. At some date which I cannot define there had arisen and continued certain rowdy activities on the early morning of Skinners' Day. The boys were released from their houses at an early hour and rushed helter-skelter to the swimming-bath where, as I understand, they all leapt into the bath simultaneously, the Head of the school diving from the highest diving board, an honour which some of these dignitaries accepted with a certain amount of trepidation. I am told that for some years after the opening of the school bathing pool this ceremonial bathe continued to be held in the allegedly sewage-stricken Medway. There was a certain appropriateness about this. It paired off with the holding of the Skinners' Day service in the parish church; for in bygone days the parish church had stood to the school's godliness as the Medway to its cleanliness, and we have on earlier pages recorded the comments of mid-Victorian *Tonbridgians* on the inadequacy of each for its purpose. Refreshed by this exploit the boys then marched down the town to the Rose and Crown and called for the Master of the Company who appeared on the top of the porch in his dressing-gown, and addressed to them a few well-chosen words. So far so good; but other and less innocent items were often added to this programme; the smashing of property and the 'ragging' of unpopular boys. The whole thing was a survival from a rowdier age when, for example, eggs were used as missiles or arguments in contested elections. In the 1933 celebration such incidents were worse than usual and the whole affair was abolished, the houses henceforth remaining locked till breakfast-time. Looking back, one is surprised that this annual festivity should have been tolerated so long.[1]

[1] In the original manuscript the seventh word from the end of this sentence

The coming of the Second Great War coincided with a change of headmasters, Mr. Sloman being succeeded by Mr. Whitworth, previously a house-master at Rugby and head-master of Bradfield. Mr. Whitworth's headmastership began with a unique event, a house-masters' meeting in the middle of the summer holidays. It is my rule in this book to say as little as possible of a personal nature about anyone still on the staff of the school, and Mr. Whitworth obviously comes within that self-denying ordinance; but as one who was present at that unique meeting I cannot forbear to say how greatly we were encouraged by the quiet confidence with which he faced the unknowable future of a school he had not yet begun to rule.

As everyone knows, the war began with an eight months' standstill on the Western front and the *Tonbridgian* of December 1939 describes the term as 'remarkably normal', its leading feature being the presence in our midst of a school much larger than ourselves—Dulwich, evacuated from South London by Government orders. The Dulwich boys had the use of our class-rooms and playing fields whenever we did not want them ourselves, thus enjoying, if that be the right word, a topsy-turvy curriculum of pleasure first and business after-wards. About fifty of the Dulwich boarders occupied the all too numerous vacancies in our boarding-houses. The rest of the school were billeted all over the town. At Christmas they returned to London.

Of course we took all kinds of precautions. At first gas masks were carried to all school periods. Then, when this began to seem absurd, we arrived at one of those curious compromises which are generally described as typically British: gas masks were not brought to school but they had to be carried 'down town' or when a boy attended any function after lock-up.

Air raids on a very small scale began immediately after the fall of France. What were we to do when the siren sounded its 'warbling note'? Obviously we were to go to the shelters which

was 'tomfoolery', but the only O.T. who read the book at this stage was pained at finding his youthful exploits thus aspersed. So here it is as you please—tomfoolery or festivity.

the Governors had thoughtfully provided for us during the year's respite after 'Munich'. According to the siren, the only available evidence, raids of many hours' duration occurred during many midsummer nights of 1940. Happily it was one of the loveliest and warmest summers on record, and these vigils, though a stuffy experience for boys cooped up in a shelter, were agreeable enough for a house-master immorally reclining in a deck-chair just outside the door, to make sure that none of his prisoners escaped.

With the summer holidays of 1940 came the real thing: the Battle of Britain and the threat of imminent invasion. Should we evacuate to Shrewsbury and suffer there, for the remainder of the war, what we had seen Dulwich suffering in our midst during the previous autumn? It is unnecessary now to schedule the arguments advanced on either side. The decision was perhaps clinched by the advice of General Ironside, himself an Old Tonbridgian and at that date Commander-in-Chief, Home Forces. He said, 'Have everything ready to go but do not go: if I find any reason to change my mind I will let you know.' So we stayed, a most fortunate decision as it turned out. Meanwhile the daylight Battle of Britain passed on into the nocturnal Battle of London, which was the chief feature of the autumn and winter of 1940-1. What were we to do about that? Night after night with hardly an exception for weeks on end the siren warbled at sundown and gave all clear at dawn. Could we really face the possibility of seven cold nights a week in shelters? Our own shelters were only sufficient for sitting accommodation, but most providentially the Dulwich visit had doubled the number of shelters, so that all could be converted, as it were, from third-class carriages into *wagons lits*. Which was it to be—*wagons lits*, migration to ground floors, or stay in bed and 'damn the consequences'? There was a difference of opinion and the headmaster allowed each house-master to go his own way. Gradually all drifted to the third solution. It was realized that Tonbridge, being a place of no military importance on the way to London and other obvious objectives, would have many sirens but few bombs and these latter probably dropped by accident. One such accidental bomb fell close to the chapel in soft mud on 20th October, 1940. It did no damage to the chapel though it smashed a few class-room windows. This was the only damage suffered by the school until the coming of the buzz-bombs in 1944.

The German planes which flew over Tonbridge on their way to London might attack the school indirectly by bombing the property there which is the source of the school's endowment. Here again the school was fortunate. The Sandhills estate lies only a little more than a mile to the north-west of St. Paul's, but little damage was done, though the rental for a time declined steeply owing to evacuation. The future prospects of the estate are said to be excellent, on account of the proximity of the new London University building. The Andrew Judde bequest is, of course, the property of the school and not of the Skinners' Company; that was settled by a lawsuit more than a hundred years ago. But the Company has other financial resources at its disposal and during the temporary financial difficulties of the school, due both to the decline in numbers and to the reduced income of the endowment, it was able to help the school from its own resources.

It must not be supposed that we ever reached a stage in which we took no notice whatever of the siren. It was ruled that the school should never continue assembled under one roof during a raid. Thus class-room work went on as usual but chapel services, other than voluntary services, and functions in Big School were abruptly terminated—another British compromise. Then there was the black-out. It was impossible to black out the chapel, so after an experiment of holding Sunday evening services in Big School during the winter terms, it was decided to return to chapel and hold the services at a time which shifted back as the hours of darkness increased, the earliest being 3.45 p.m.

The war, of course, brought with it new obligations—emergency agriculture, or more correctly horticulture, Home Guard and domestic duties; for most of the boarding-houses were at one time or another short of domestic staff. The football field off the Shipbourne road to the north of 'the Fifty' was delivered over to agriculture, or horticulture, under the supervision of Mr. Thomas, and there were house allotments on Martin's.

Mr. Thomas has supplied me with some particulars about the school's farming effort during the war, from which it appears that the ex-rugby football ground in the Shipbourne road produced during four years 62 tons of potatoes, 17 tons of cabbages, 10 tons of swede turnips and over 1 ton of brussels sprouts. He adds: 'One of the indirect gains has been a definite stimulation of interest in agriculture, illustrated by requests for books on the subject for the school library.' It is certainly true that many more boys than formerly show a keen interest in farming and what appears to the present ignorant writer a considerable technical knowledge of the subject. This is probably true of other schools and is a feature of the spirit of the age. Maybe, it is largely due to the fact that farmers have prospered during the war and more of them are sending their sons to public schools.

Service in the Home Guard, for boys over seventeen, was regarded by some of us as an unnecessary imposition on boys and masters who were already doing their military 'bit' in J.T.C. or A.T.C., especially as the boy members would presumably be dispersed to their homes by any event which called the Home Guard into action. However, the school contingent of the H.G. performed various nocturnal duties at various times, and one of the headmaster's Skinners' Day reports refers to 'boys who, after the Postern patrol, take their breakfast like gentlemen at ten o'clock'. Our schoolboy Home Guards never encountered the enemy but on one occasion they were attacked by two intoxicated allies. These allies retired hurt, one of them on a stretcher.

Shortage of staff at 'the Grubber' was at one time acute. Masters and their wives came to its assistance, and on certain days it was possible, during the break, to buy a dough bun from the headmaster. What would Dr. Welldon, the centenary of whose first term was celebrated in 1943 by a whole holiday and a most interesting address from Sir Cyril Norwood, have thought of that?

The numbers of the school, which had fallen from 470 to 400 in the last three years of Mr. Sloman's headmastership, continued their descent until 1941 when they reached 306. Then when the worst of the bombing appeared to be over, though the tide of war itself had not yet decisively turned, they began to rise again, first slowly and then rapidly. By the end of the war the school had again over 400 boys and was in fact full and turning away applicants, for its powers of accommodation had been reduced. Park House was closed in 1940 and Ferox Hall rather more than a year later. Park House remained in partial occupation by the Smythe House day boys, whose premises had become a first-aid post. Ferox was let to the Kent County Home for the Aged. The downward curve of numbers was specially sharp at Tonbridge for obvious geographical reasons but it was experienced in a greater or lesser degree by most boarding-schools. So long as the bombing danger was acute many parents preferred to have their boys at home, and those who dislike the public schools imagined that their day was over and that most of them would soon be liquidated in the bankruptcy court. But it was not to be so. The revival has been as widespread as the decline. The remarkable increase in the boarding-school population may be attributed to a number of causes: shortage of domestic servants in the homes, over-worked mothers and absent fathers, restriction of expenditure in other directions such as motor cars, and so on. War, it seems, apart from bombing, is favourable to boarding-schools, for their experience in the last war was the same.

However that may be, few or none were so optimistic as to forecast that both the closed houses would be re-opened within four or five years of their closure, Park House under Mr. Hoole in 1944 and Ferox Hall under Mr. McNeill in 1946.

The maxim 'business as usual' is a bad guide for a nation's industrial system in wartime but it is not altogether inapplicable as an unattainable ideal for schools. The purpose of schools is the education of the young and, whereas the manufacture of peace-time luxuries can be postponed, the education of the young cannot. The Greek word from which our English word 'school' is derived actually means 'leisure'—mysterious and ironic equation in an age when school education even in peace-time has come to consist of 'one damned thing after another', organized this and organized that, a jumble and a scramble and a passing of examinations. The leisure implied by the Greek is not of course idleness but we may assume that it implies a free-dom of the mind and of the soul from ephemeral distractions. Certainly the headmaster, while readily accepting on behalf of the school its duty to contribute to the cause of the moment, by wartime extras of one sort and another, always kept in view the school's primary duty, not merely to its boys and their parents but to the post-war world, namely, to provide, so far as might be, conditions of 'leisure' in which education could be ade-quately carried on.

Not the least of these considerations was the recruitment of the staff. The natural wastage of old age continued to take its course, many of the younger members went on active service, and the normal field of recruitment was closed. In this depart-ment we were extremely fortunate and it might be main-tained that in some important respects the staff was a better one at the end of the war that it had been at the beginning. Mr. Harvey Adams brought a flood of new ideas and enthus-iasms into the art department, and Dr. Bunney set in immedi-ate motion a renaissance of music. It was very fortunate that just when Shakespearian drama suffered an eclipse through the retirement of Arnold, music stepped in to fill the gap with a valiant amateur orchestra and admirable performances of the great choral works of Handel, Bach, Mozart and Brahms. It may be worth recording that, in the middle of the war, the house instrumental music competition, hitherto an obscure and *in camera* affair, was remodelled on lines suggested by Sir George Dyson. Each house now gives a fifteen minutes' con-cert which all who like may listen to, if only for the satisfaction of disagreeing with the subsequent award of the adjudicator.

All the new members of the staff were not permanencies and in the latter category were four ladies, one of whom established her position promptly and decisively by defeating the captain

6. THE STAFF 1945

NAMES (LEFT TO RIGHT): SEATED: *P. L. Bathurst, J. N. F. Morris, D. C. Somervell, K. T. Gemmell, H. S. Vere Hodge, E. E. A. Whitworth, G. L. Herman, E. J. H. Eames, T. Staveley, G. P. Hoole, C. H. Knott;* STANDING (LOWER ROW): *A. L. Thomas, Col. A. Latham, Rev. F. H. Gripper, Z. Lubienski, R. H. P. Reiss, V. Hedley Jones, H. M. Gray, Hervey Adams, J. M. McNeill, J. C. Stredder, B. C. M. Dixon, L. W. Stephens;* BACK ROW: *R. T. Christie, W. P. Lake, F. W. Tugwell, Mrs. Tugwell, Miss Blundell, Miss D. Yeats Brown, Miss Jarvis, A. W. Bunney, W. A. L. Hill, C. Bullock*

of the cricket eleven at squash rackets. The question whether, in normal times and on general principles, a co-educational staff would be a good thing for a boys' school—or a girls' school—might well be discussed by educationists. (I believe most members of my own sex believe that such a staff would be good for a girls' school and bad for a boys' school; but let that pass.) What will not be contested is that, in wartime, a good lady-master is preferable to a bad gentleman-master, and if the reader jib at the term 'lady-master' I must call his attention to the fact that a Tonbridge boy astonished his parents by writing home 'I have two mistresses this term'.

One of the consequences of the war was the promotion of the natural sciences, physics and chemistry, to a clear predominance over the other lines of study, classics and modern languages, which between the two wars had competed with each other and with science on more or less equal terms. Both the wars exerted a pressure in this direction, for reasons which we will not attempt to analyse. Before the first war a classical education was the norm, and both modern side and science side were departures from it, deliberately selected for definite reasons, vocational or otherwise. During the Second War a scientific education became the norm, and the science side was as overloaded with boys with no real aptitude for science as the classical side used to be overloaded with boys with no real aptitude for classics. The classical side is 'winnowed and sifted and brought to a handful', as Cromwell said of the Long Parliament after all but the good members—that is, those who agreed with him—had been excluded. Its three forms number barely twenty, all told, the majority of them are winners of entrance scholarships. The modern side also has shrunk, in reality if not in appearance, for about half its members do not do German. It has become, in effect, a combined modern languages, modern history and English literature side, and there is evidence that the offer of a 'modern' curriculum without German is already reducing the wartime pressure on the science side. In these respects the course of events at Tonbridge is presumably much the same as the course of events in all other public schools.

In June 1944, when we assumed that the worst of the blitz was long over and done with, came the buzz-bombs, or doodle-bugs, and deranged our routine more extensively than ever before; for the sirens proved unable to give adequate warning of the approach of these monsters and quickly gave up the attempt to do so. For the last six weeks of that summer term daily morning chapel was dropped and the Sunday services became voluntary—for we had long established the compromise, typically British no doubt, that voluntary gatherings could continue during an air raid whereas compulsory assemblies of the whole school could not. There was no Skinners' Day, for the first time presumably in the history of the school, though a quasi-Skinners' Day was held in the following March to enable the master of the year to deliver his address to the school. At about 10 p.m. on June 23rd a buzz-bomb fell in a tennis court on the north side of Bordyke and innumerable windows were shattered in the school buildings. Doors also were rent off hinges but not a single injury requiring hospital treatment was suffered by any inhabitant of School House. The other houses were for the most part unaffected, though Manor House had an even narrower escape from destruction on another occasion. The next morning's school was cancelled to enable the boys to assist in clearing up the wreckage and it seems that a good time was had by all.

The war ended on the third day of the following summer term. The day was proclaimed a whole holiday, and as most boys went home everything passed off very quietly, though there were some orderly and well-behaved little bonfires on the Upper Hundred in the evening. Our reactions to victories seem to be in inverse proportion to their magnitude. We made less noise over the downfall of Nazidom than over Armistice Day 1918 and far less than over the relief of Mafeking in 1900. At the beginning of June the school was granted a three days' exeat. Most boys considered that this was such a success that it ought to become an annual event. *Dis aliter visum*—which means 'the authorities disagreed with them'.

And so on to the first Skinners' Day of this post-war world

from which some hope and others fear so much. More than a hundred years have passed since the governors used to drive down from London by coach, as shown in the delightful steel engraving which hangs in the Masters' Common Room. More than twenty years since the Master and his Wardens were driven from the Rose and Crown to the school in an open landau by Old Morley, that Methuselah of cabbies—for he is still alive. None the less they arrive, and at 10.30 a.m. we see them advancing towards us where we stand awaiting them under the clock tower. They do not afford quite as dazzling an exhibition of the sartorial art as in the days when I first remember them. The head of the school, a scientist, reads the Latin Oration which Mr. Vere Hodge has kindly composed for him. 'O Pelliparii . . .' It bristles with ingenious witticisms and topical allusions. The school has been told where to laugh. Some of the governors look as if they understood it all; others —but of course they all understand it. The senior examiner, generally a Fellow of All Souls College, Oxford, replies in another Latin speech, which is more difficult to follow because we have not got it in print before us. Then we troop into Big School where the Master is going to tell the boys what he has been thinking about lately, and his thoughts are not screened from us by the decent obscurity of a learned tongue. Happily he cannot moralize on the atomic bomb, for three weeks have yet to elapse before it will be dropped. In fact the war is not quite over after all. After this function we proceed to the parish church, where our predecessors endured every Sunday the mild agonies described in an earlier chapter, and listen to the beautiful Bidding Prayer with which this book opens.

Before bringing this history to a close, I must wave a friendly farewell to the *Tonbridgian*, which has been my constant guide and companion through the last eighty-eight years of the school's history, and indeed through very much the greater part of this book. We have already noticed that the two Great Wars, as one would expect, influenced the development of the school in much the same way. But the *Tonbridgian* itself offers an exception to this rule. In the latter half of the first war our periodical swelled to unprecedented dimensions owing to the indefatigable energy of Mr. Stokoe in accumulating information about O.T.'s on active service. In the latter part of the second war the fiat of the paper controller reduced it to a mere shadow of its natural self, coverless and printed in microscopic type. Only in the first post-war issue was it allowed to reclothe itself and put on weight.

If, ruling out the war years as exceptional, we compare the paper as it is in modern times with its mid-Victorian youth, we cannot fail to observe a change which is perhaps not altogether for the better. What it was like in its early days we have already said; it might be described, by an adaptation of Lincoln's words, as a production of schoolboys by schoolboys for schoolboys; it was naïve, amateurish, outspoken and controversial. To-day it is more of an official organ; there are columns of records more interesting to O.T.'s than to present members of the school. It also contains complicated balance sheets of amalgamated funds and other beneficent institutions which cause mere mortals to turn over the page in haste. Naïvely controversial letters from crudely critical schoolboys, recording schoolboy opinion, seldom appear. The intellectual aristocracy occasionally favour us with their masterpieces of verse and prose but the 'boy in the street' no longer makes himself audible in these columns. But we would not part with our authority on a note of criticism. Without the *Tonbridgian* this book could not have been written.

We have done; for we do not intend to offer any remarks on that much-discussed problem, the future of the public schools. We will only say this. If history teaches one thing more plainly than another, it is that nothing that is alive stands still. For two hundred and ninety years, from John Proctor to Thomas Knox, Tonbridge School was something entirely unlike what it has since, for a mere hundred years, been, yet it went on doing its job, sometimes better and sometimes worse, and produced a number of useful servants of the community. Then it began to change, and went on changing rapidly in a changing and expanding world. The world will continue to change, if not to expand. Indeed we are told that the boy population of this island has for some time past been shrinking and will inevitably continue to shrink for some time to come, though it may be that that shrinkage will be offset, so far as the public schools are concerned, by the fact of an increasing percentage of a diminishing total being sent to boarding-schools, at the expense either of their own parents or of the community in general. These are hazardous speculations. In any case, may the school, whatever its size and whatever its character, maintain its quality and do—for none can do more—its best.

APPENDIX

For those who like statistics I give the numbers in the school during the last hundred years, as printed in *Annual Report of the Old Tonbridgian Society*, inserting the names of the headmasters. The figures up to 1893 are for Skinners' Day, and after that for January. The distinction is unimportant, though schools, if not automatically 'full', are generally fuller in July than in January.

Dr. Welldon	Dr. Tancock	1914—403	1932—467
1845—139	1898—433	1915—383	1933—451
1851—129	1899—400	1916—366	1934—476
1855—110	1900—398	1917—400	1935—474
1860—182	1901—362	1918—444	1936—467
1865—178	1902—361	1919—452	1937—457
1870—214	1903—382	1920—471	1938—411
1875—239	1904—381	1921—474	1939—400
	1905—394	1922—474	
Mr. Rowe	1906—400		Mr.
1880—209	1907—402		Whitworth
1885—216		Mr. Sloman	1940—374
1890—175	Mr. Lowry	1923—485	1941—319
	1908—390	1924—488	1942—306
Dr. Wood	1909—416	1925—486	1943—326
1891—278	1910—426	1926—487	1944—365
1892—328	1911—446	1927—495	1945—405
1893—365	1912—436	1928—491	1946—440
1896—411	1913—436	1929—492	
1897—441		1930—494	
		1931—469	

The reader can make his own deductions, but he may like a few comments. As there were only forty-three boys in the school in Dr. Welldon's first term he tripled its numbers in his first three years. Thereafter the rise was uncertain and slow for fifteen years but his last ten years, years of great prosperity for the upper classes of the whole country, show a substantial increase.

The decline under Mr. Rowe was mainly due to the fact that the age of entry tended to advance rapidly and the school ceased to be a 'prep school and public school combined', i.e. the number of boys of what would now be considered public school age probably remained constant.

The sudden increase of 100 in Dr. Wood's first year was due to the influx from Leamington, but the school continued to increase at an average rate of thirty boys a year throughout his headmastership.

Dr. Tancock's reign shows a relapse and a recovery. Mr. Lowry's shows a steady rise, apart from the relapse, experienced probably by most other schools, during the first half of the 1914-18 war. During Mr. Sloman's time numbers continued to grow slowly to a maximum of 494 in 1930, the year when the great slump began. Thereafter they declined slowly, but the decline was not serious until his last two years.

Mr. Whitworth's arrival coincided with the outbreak of the Second Great War and this inevitably brought a steep decline. Considering the geographical position of the school it is perhaps surprising that the decline was not more catastrophic, and that the recovery set in so quickly.

INDEX

149

INDEX